SEVEN SUMMITS OF SUCCESS

SEVEN SUMMITS OF SUCCESS

ROBERT HELLER & REBECCA STEPHENS

Published in 2005 by Capstone Publishing Limited (a Wiley Company), The Atrium, Southern Gate Chichester, West Sussex, PO19 8SQ, England
Phone (+44) 1243 779777

Email (for orders and customer service enquires): cs-books@wiley.co.uk
Visit our Home Page on www.wiley.co.uk or www.wiley.com

Robert Heller and Rebecca Stephens have asserted their right under the Copyright, Designs and Patents Act 1988, to be identified as the authors of this work.

Other Wiley Editorial Offices

John Wiley & Sons, Inc. 111 River Street, Hoboken, NJ 07030, USA
Jossey-Bass, 989 Market Street, San Francisco, CA 94103-1741, USA
Wiley-VCH Verlag GmbH, Pappellaee 3, D-69469 Weinheim, Germany
John Wiley & Sons Australia, Ltd, 33 Park Road, Milton, Queensland, 4064, Australia
John Wiley & Sons (Asia) Pte Ltd, 2 Clementi Loop #02-01, Jin Xing Distripark, Singapore 129809
John Wiley & Sons Canada Ltd, 22 Worcester Road, Etobicoke, Ontario, Canada, M9W 1L1

Wiley also publishes its books in a variety of electronic formats. Some content that appears in print may not be available in electronic books.

Library of Congress Cataloging-in-Publication Data is available

British Library Cataloguing in Publication Data

A catalogue record for this book is available from the British Library

ISBN 1841126594

Typeset in Agfa Rotis Sans Serif by Sparks (www.sparks.co.uk)

Printed and bound by CPI Antony Rowe, Eastbourne

Contents

Prologue

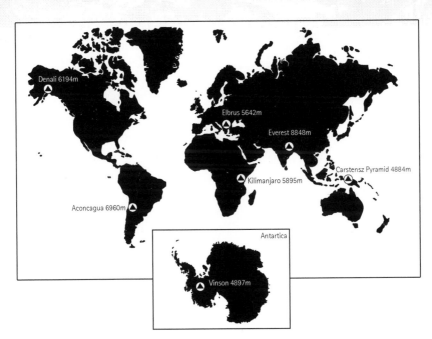

The Seven Summits are the highest peaks in each of the seven continents. They are Kilimanjaro (Africa); Denali (North America); Everest (Asia); Elbrus (Europe); Carstensz Pyramid (Australasia); Aconcagua (South America) and Vinson (Antarctica). They represent seven supreme challenges for ambitious climbers. Like them, everyone has seven supreme tests to pass on their way to the top – if they truly want to get there.

People fall into three broad, overlapping groups: first, the achievers and under-achievers; second, the ambitious and unambitious; and third, the able and the unable. Able people who fall short of their achievement potential through lack of ambition are wasting precious talent. Even among the achievers, however, few truly live up to their full potential. The best of them know this to be so. For them, there's always another, higher mountain to climb.

So there is for *everybody*. The unable can learn new abilities. The unambitious can discover and develop constructive desires. This book tells how to find and achieve the new heights that are within your reach, even when the peaks seem most daunting. Our argument is not theoretical. It describes and illuminates a crucial fact of real life for individuals and organizations.

One of Japan's supreme post-war leaders, Ryuzaburo Kaku, based an astonishing career on the mountaineering metaphor. He took over at Canon when this small maker of high-class cameras and other optical gear was in mortal danger. Kaku overrode the threats and seized the opportunities as he set about 'climbing Mount Fuji' – creating a premier Japanese company.

When I interviewed Kaku in the 1980s, the great man was 'climbing Mount Everest'. Now, he said, Canon had to become 'a premier world company' – and Kaku also achieved that improbable ambition. My many studies of business heroes, from oil titan John D.Rockefeller in the 1860s to Microsoft's Bill Gates in the late twentieth century, have shown the same pattern of unstoppable upward drive built on the foundations of intelligent, high voltage aspiration and strong, aware self-management.

Rebecca Stephens understands the force of Kaku's metaphor better than all but a few people. She has climbed the actual Mount Everest – the first British woman to do so. And she went on climbing until she had scaled all Seven Summits – again, the first British woman to complete this formidable series. She knows as an individual what it takes in ambition, know-how, persistence and endurance to scale the highest challenges in the world. That has given her special insight into the attributes and actions behind the feats of brilliant achievers – people like the tycoons mentioned above.

Rebecca and I first met as co-speakers at an event organized by Will Carling, then England rugby captain, and no mean achiever himself. Carling's in-company seminars embodied a strong belief about champion athletes (like Adrian Moorhouse, the Olympic gold medal swimmer, and the marvellous runner Sebastian Coe, as well as Carling). The belief is that top-level sport has important lessons to teach business people.

Just as I have developed my own insights further with each successive book, from *The Naked Manager* to *The Fusion Manager*, so Rebecca Stephens has built up her ideas, not only in completing the arduous Seven Summits, but through her subsequent speaking and writing. Each of the climbs, we discovered, drew on different, specific, but interlocking areas of applied personality and intellect. Each vital factor proved to have a direct analogy with the key areas of organizational and personal management. Mastering the *Seven Summits of Success* thus provides a powerful toolkit with which people can achieve the aims on which they have set their hearts.

But there's the drawback. Few people are entirely without any ambition at all. That has to be especially true in business, where naming and achieving objectives is supposedly the fundamental process. But even in business the majority lack focus. They plan neither for their own advancement, nor for defined, ambitious success in their areas of responsibility. Even if they do form ambitions, what's more, they undershoot, under-estimating both their strengths and their ability to go well beyond their present horizons.

If Canon's Kaku and other post-war Japanese tycoons had stuck within their apparent limitations, resting on top of Mount Fuji, they would have missed out on their Everests – the unfamiliar markets of western industries where they had little or no competitive experience. Likewise, the common factor behind all the great entrepreneurs is their boldness, not in taking risks (which, like good mountaineers, they seek to minimize or avoid entirely), but in trusting their own capabilities.

Offered the chance to bid for the operating system for IBM's nascent personal computer, the very young Bill Gates was undeterred by his lack of anything to sell the giant: he just bought the system that became MS-DOS from a less aware company down the road in Seattle – and got a flying start towards his personal, unprecedented peak.

The object of this book is to awaken readers to their self-imposed restrictions, which hold back their ability and ambition – and thus their achievement; to show how they can transcend past and present to achieve a far more satisfying and successful future; and to inspire them, having achieved a new and dynamic mindset, to turn thought into effective action. The saga of the *Seven Summits of Success* is about having the desire and the courage to pursue your own chosen path – to climb your own Everest. That may prove to involve a complex route. But the climber's basic question is simple.

WHERE DO I WANT MYSELF/THE BUSINESS TO BE IN X YEARS' TIME?

Simple, yes. Yet the effort of looking for the answer is too much for too many people – even though the search process in itself takes you a long way towards the destination. A study of one Princeton graduating class showed that only 3% of the grads had a clear idea of what they wanted to achieve. Follow-up revealed that this tiny minority went on to achieve more, in terms of personal wealth, than all their contemporaries put together.

Once you have found your objective, desire or dream (whatever you want to call it), that vision will act as your lodestar, your guiding light, the benchmark against which you can test all your decisions and actions as you climb your personal mountains. Realizing the dream involves two further, harder questions:

WHERE AM I NOW?
HOW DO I GET FROM HERE TO WHERE I WANT TO BE?

The tough part of the first question is being totally, ruthlessly honest. The easiest part of the latter question is: How do I start? By just starting is the simple answer. While on Everest for a journalistic assignment, Rebecca Stephens became so involved in the venture she was reporting, and in the challenge facing the climbers, that she set herself a target, too – to climb to Camp 1. It was far from easy, but she did it:

'Something profound changed in me that day ... for the first time in my 27 years, I could clearly define what it was that I wanted to do ... I wanted to climb Mount Everest.'

This was a literally lofty ambition for a woman with no experience. High ambitions always need confirmation by experience. Rebecca's ascent of Mount Kilimanjaro in Tanzania was the first stage in confirming that the Everest plan was no fantasy. It provides the first analogy, illuminating the first of the Seven Summits of Management that must be mastered for success. The full seven are:

1   Seize the moment of opportunity

2   Develop the indispensable skills

3   Master creative teamwork

4   Become expert in true leadership

5   Work with the best available talent

6   Use the power of positive thinking

7   Keep right on to the end of the road.

This book is built around seven chapters, each using one of the seven mountains as starting point before expanding to include theory and practice in the relevant area of management summitry. The chapters are designed to deliver powerful and inspiring lessons from which every manager (however far from the summits now) and every organization (however small now) can profit on the upward climb to their highest present ambitions – and beyond. The final chapter describes how to master the next and possibly best stage: what to do for an encore.

Acknowledgements

This book has many co-authors, who may not be aware of their part in its writing, but have none the less been invaluable. Rebecca and I first met, for example, under the aegis of Will Carling, whose management courses were exploring and exploiting the power of analogies between sporting achievement and managerial success. What Carling had learnt as Captain of the England Rugby XV, which was expounded in our book *The Way to Win*, was augmented by the experiences of several other sportsmen and women – including Rebecca.

What began on a shared platform, speaking for Will, would not, however, have resulted in the current book without the later, timely intervention of our mutual agent, Derek Johns of A.P.Watt. He saw the opportunity, acted as midwife to the project and provided unfailing support all the way to fruition. On my side of the enterprise, business management, that fruition was only possible because of the stimulating material gleaned from publications such as *Business Week*, *Fortune* and in particular the *Harvard Business Review*, whose admirable contributors are acknowledged in the text.

I also learnt much from recent assignments, especially the Ideas Audits commissioned by the East of England Development Agency. A brilliant idea in itself, on which EEDA and its advisers, Omobono Ltd, deserve every congratulation, this project introduced me to three companies, Charles Wells, ARM and HFL, which exemplify the nature and possibilities of management summitry in an age of super-abundant opportunity.

I also owe a great debt to colleagues such as Simon Caulkin, management editor of the *Observer*; Edward de Bono, my collaborator on the monthly *Letter to Thinking Managers*; Sally Smith and her team at John Wiley; Anjali Pratap at A.P.Watt; my patient assistant, Aine O'Shaughnessy; fellow-members of the Global Future Forum; and my friends at Dorling Kindersley for engaging me for their *Essential Managers* and the *Business Mastermind* series, most of whose high-climbing heroes (Peter Drucker, Bill Gates, Jack Welch, Andy Grove, Charles Handy, Tom Peters and Warren Buffett) feature in these pages.

Robert Heller

Adding to the above, writes Rebecca, I would like to thank all those who assisted me both mentally and physically up those mountains, and whose names, in the main, appear between the covers of this book. In particular, though, thanks are due to Roger Mear, who first invited me to Everest and unwittingly, perhaps, opened my eyes to a pastime that was to completely turn about my life; and to John Barry, who taught me all that I know about mountaineering. Also to Dave Halton for giving up his chance to climb Aconcagua to look after our sick companion (and whose photo, taken on Vinson, appears on the front cover of this book), to Graham McMahon for dragging me up Carstensz Pyramid, and to Lucy Hannah and Fiona Gately for making their respective climbs such good fun. And to the Sherpas, of course – in particular Chhwang, Ang Passang, Kami Tcheri and Tcheri Zhambu – who enabled me to climb Everest and who I shall thank until the end of my days.

That's not to forget Peter Earl, who instigated the Everest expedition and successfully secured the funds, and all the companies and individuals who supported us, in particular the whisky people at Glenmorangie who wrote the first sponsorship cheque and gave us hope, and our principal sponsor, DHL International UK Ltd, which funded not only Everest, but also Elbrus, Carstensz Pyramid, Aconcagua and Vinson.

And lastly, to add to those at A.P.Watt and John Wiley who orchestrated the production of this book, my boyfriend, Jovan, who learnt all about the pressure of deadlines and kept his cool.

Rebecca Stephens

Defining the Dream 1

It isn't often that we get the chance to escape the office for a ten-week break, but the opportunity came my way and I grabbed it. In 1989, I was working for a small, specialist magazine for English-speaking expatriates, when I took a call from a British climber, Roger Mear. He and one other British climber, together with a small band of climbers from Seattle, were off to climb Everest's North East Ridge. Would I like to join them as a reporter?

'Well, yes!' I didn't pause for breath. And then was fortunate that a chat over lunch with the editor of our parent newspaper, the *Financial Times*, secured a commission for a series of articles. 'I'd like to know what is base camp,' he insisted. 'We all know the term, but what do people do there? What do they eat? What do they talk about?'

It was a layman's viewpoint he was after, and I couldn't have been better positioned to provide it, for at the time I knew very little about mountains, virtually nothing about mountaineering, and less, if that were possible, about mountaineers.

On reflection, I couldn't possibly have foreseen how completely this assignment to the Himalayas was going to turn my life around. But even in the moment, in the living out of the experience, it proved to be an especially joyous and enriching time. I was 27 years old and my eyes were opened wide as if a student again. Everything was fresh, everything new – and much of it exquisitely beautiful.

One late afternoon, journeying on the road from Kathmandu, north towards the Friendship Bridge and the Tibetan border, the driver of our dilapidated bus stopped short of our proposed destination because of the failing light. It was raining, too, great rivulets of water washing the mud from beneath the wheels of the bus. We stepped out into the wet and up a flight of wooden steps curling around the back of a small wooden teahouse. A lamp beckoned inside and we were led to a small room: three bunks pushed against the walls, a low table with a single candle on a small, chipped saucer, and a window, of sorts. It was a simple, square hole cut in the wood, no glass, and shutters, open to the night.

The rain lashed down on the roof tiles and the smell of the surrounding vegetation infiltrated the room with such forcefulness that, with our eyes shut, we might have been excused for thinking we were lying on the forest floor itself. And there we slept, fully clothed, with a quilt to provide the comfort of a little weight on our tired limbs, until dawn broke and we set out on our way again.

It instilled in me a sense of freedom that was only to be magnified at Everest's base camp and beyond. Here, with no responsibilities other than to write an article or two, I would wander the moraine banks of the East and Central Rongbuk Glaciers with little concern about the passing of time, knowing that if I didn't make camp I could always roll out my bivouac bag and sleep exactly where I found myself.

It was in sharp contrast to the tightly scheduled working and social environs of home, and I found it immensely attractive. I liked the simplicity of life away from the telephone and nagging deadlines. I liked the challenge of making myself at home, and comfortable, with no more than could be jammed into a single rucksack. And more than anything, I liked where I found myself, surrounded by the highest mountains in the world.

There is, of course, an austerity to the landscape at high altitudes: barren rock, and ice; the colours, taupe, beige, brown, white, blue. No green to give any hope of life. And yet there is clarity of light – a filter of heavy atmosphere lifted from the air – that razor-sharpens edges and draws distant ridges impossibly near. And there's the scale of things: a vastness that makes one feel at once humbly insignificant and, paradoxically, acutely alive and confident of one's place in the world. I had never felt better in my life. Only one thing made me feel a little displaced in this new world I had happened upon, and that was my companions – or more accurately, my companions' focus and palpable passion to climb Everest.

There must have been at least a hundred climbers at the base camp on Everest's northern reaches that year – plus several tens of Sherpas climbing in support – and with the exception of a few Tibetan yak herders, an expedition doctor or two and one other journalist, every one of them was there with the sole purpose of climbing this mountain.

Did they know the sacrifices they were making? Or, indeed, the risks to life and limb? I soon learned that few of these climbers held down steady jobs or family lives. And who could be surprised? It surely couldn't be much fun for those left at home, holding the fort in Tokyo, or Bulgaria, or the Lake District, incommunicado for months at a time (this was before the days of satellite communication), without knowing if their loved ones were alive or dead. For the reality is that death is far from being a rare event in the high mountains. From the early reconnaissance expeditions in the 1920s, when seven Sherpas lost their lives, to the present day, people die high on Everest with tragic regularity. Whatever climbers say, it *is* more dangerous than crossing the road.

So why do climbers risk their all in the quest to scale an oversized lump of rock? Why do climbers climb? I had been around these people long enough, puzzled but also impressed by their focus, that I wanted to know the answer to this question. And there was only one way to find out: to climb myself.

At the point when this idea struck me I had already been once to a camp the climbers dubbed ABC – advanced base camp. ABC is at an altitude of 6,450m (21,160ft) and although a mere 1,300m (4,265ft) higher than the base camp, it is thirteen *horizontal* miles from the latter – a long old slog along the lateral moraine of the East Rongbuk Glacier and exhausting for mountaineer and journalist alike. Nonetheless, if I were to add that yaks, too, bearing loads of camping, cooking and oxygen apparatus make the same journey on four delicate hooves, it will be clear that there is nothing on the journey that might be classified as technical.

It was no surprise, then, to any of the climbers on the expedition, that I might join them to this point – or that I might return a second time to ABC, as was my plan. But to go higher? That was a different matter.

'They'll think you mad at home', muttered Tim, one of the American climbers. Perched on a couple of rocks, we looked out from the camp, across the upper reaches of the East Rongbuk Glacier towards the first feature on the North East Ridge: Bill's Buttress. The buttress rises straight from the level plains of the glacier at a rakish angle of some 40° for about 680m (2,230ft). At its apex the angle of the ridge changes, like a refracted beam of light, and continues in a diagonal sweep over a cluster of saw-toothed pinnacles towards the summit.

Bill's Buttress, in effect, is the first step onto the North East Ridge. At the top of this step the climbers had pitched a single tent: Camp 1. This, I decided, was to be my goal, my 'summit'. At 7,125m (23,380ft) it was a long way from the true summit at 8,848m (29,028ft), but it was high enough to feel the debilitating effects of altitude, and steep enough – on mixed ground of snow and rock – to try out some technical climbing, albeit at an elementary level.

'You'll be on your own, kid', Tim added. 'Fall sick up there and there'll be no one in any state to help you down.'

This wasn't news that I welcomed. Only the day before Tim had been encouraging. He was the one who had taken the trouble to teach me the ropes, literally as it happens: how to *jumar* up them using a friction device, and abseil down, full body-weight leaning out from the mountain.

But I realized quickly enough that it wasn't the technical side of things that gave him concern. His reticence was because of the altitude. He was spelling out the risks to me as a surgeon might to a patient prior to undertaking an operation. There was mountain sickness to consider, he pointed out, and pulmonary oedema. Even cerebral oedema. Frostbite and hypothermia, too.

'I'm trying to help, that's all', he said. 'You should think about it.'

Well, I did.

'So you're climbing to Camp 1?' chipped in Chhwang, the lead Sherpa on our expedition.

'I suppose so', I said.

'Then you'll need kit.'

This was a small point that I had overlooked. I had fleeces and a pair of leather walking boots – my first, bought especially for the trip – and a ski jacket borrowed from a friend, but that was it.

Chhwang was heading down to base camp, his rucksack already packed. But now he was ferreting deep inside and emptying its contents onto the rocks. 'Here', he said, handing me his plastic mountain boots and his crampons, his harness and his ice-axe. 'I wish I was climbing with you.'

A few days passed before I mustered the energy to put into action what I had set out in my mind to do. I was only just learning about the effects of altitude but at 6,450m (21,160ft) the oxygen levels in the air are considerably reduced – less than half that at sea level. There were days when I felt I could bounce from my makeshift home in the store tent, and others when I could barely lift my body off the floor – in large part due to a subtle swing in barometric pressure.

There was one morning, though, when the barometer swung in our favour – and the sun shone, too. Tim, who I might have climbed with, had already made his way to

Camp 1, and it was with another of the Americans, Kurt, that I roped up and stepped off the moraine and onto the glacier.

It was a surprising place to be – like nowhere I had been before. Empty. Silent, but for the crunching of our own footsteps through the snow. Before long we had left the camp far behind, and the glacier stretched out before us in every direction, like a vast white sheet, a nothingness, but for long, oblong crevasses that lay dark and silent in the snow.

After a short while we had crossed the glacier and stood at the foot of Bill's Buttress. This is where the test began. The climbers had already fixed rope the length of the ridge from bottom to top. We clipped our *jumars* onto the rope. Kurt set off and I followed, deliberately placing one cramponed boot in the deep bucket steps he kicked in the snow, and then another.

Progress was good at the start. As the sun climbed in the sky so we climbed higher, each incremental gain in height rewarded with an ever more bewildering view as one distant Himalayan peak popped up behind another, each gleaming a blinding white in the sunshine.

But things change all too quickly in the mountains, as I was to learn. One minute we were squinting into the sunlight; the next, snow was falling in large puffed-up flakes around us, masking our vision and chilling us to the core. The ground was steep. The air was uncomfortably thin; such that I was forced to rest, catch breath, regroup, with every step. And there was no view, no inspiration to struggle on – just a cold, silent greyness, punctuated by the eerie rumbling of avalanches sloughing off unseen slopes.

Alone, I have no doubt that I would have turned about in my steps and clung tight to the ropes all the way back down to camp. The effort to keep going was enormous. Even within twenty metres of our tent – our refuge – I leaned back in my harness and rested on the rope for ten minutes or more, before I could finally muster the energy for the last few paces. But, after seven hours of battling with gravity, heaving the weight of our bodies against its force, we made it.

Tim, my tutor, was in the tent awaiting our arrival. He had been attempting to blaze a trail beyond Camp 1 towards the Pinnacles, but was taking a break for a while, due to a fresh, heavy dump of snow. I collapsed into the tent and beamed a smile that might have cracked my face in two. The relief, the unabashed pride I felt in having elevated myself to this isolated, lofty place, was overwhelming.

Tim passed me a mug of sweetened milk, a square of chocolate, and the flavours burst on my tongue in a rush. Every sense, it seemed, was heightened; everything intensified. I sat on the floor of the tent, looking out into the greyness and falling snow, up a broad ridge burdened with a heavy caking of snow, towards the Pinnacles. Beyond them was the highest point on Earth. How, I marvelled, had I found myself here?

REFLECTIONS

Looking back, that day on Bill's Buttress was an experience unparalleled in my life: the remoteness and beauty, the pushing of physical limits, the extreme turns in the weather, the relief and the sheer, unadulterated joy. I have a photograph of myself, sitting outside the tent at 7,125m (23,380ft), smiling, with snowflakes falling across my face and in my hair. I look unreservedly delighted to be there.

But that venture onto Everest's North East Ridge was more than a good day out. Something profound changed in me that day. Firstly, in the doing, I had an answer to my question, 'why do climbers climb?' More than that, indeed: it seemed that I, too, had been bitten by the mountaineering bug and wanted more.

And secondly – more importantly – it triggered a sequence of thoughts that led me to know for the first time in my life exactly what it was that I wanted to do. Somewhere on Bill's Buttress – whistling down the ropes, or lolloping polar bear-like in the fresh, thigh-deep snow on the lower slopes – a germ of an idea was hatched. I wanted to climb Mount Everest – an ambition that in time was to lead to a further ambition: to climb the Seven Summits.

To climb Everest was a bold ambition, perhaps, for one who had climbed only a single day in her life. But one that in the course of a few weeks, or months, I felt with complete conviction. I had discovered something that I loved, and this I believed – in my innocence, perhaps – was enough to drive me to acquire the requisite skills and make it happen.

As an abserver on that first expedition I was already beginning to make a few suppositions about what it took to climb the highest mountain in the world. Nobody reached the summit that year. The snow was so plentiful, so deep, that it proved impossible for the climbers to wade through it at extreme altitude. In the mountains, as in life, there are some things outside our control. But nonetheless it was clear to me that those climbers who reached the loftiest points weren't necessarily those who were equipped with the fittest body, or who were the most competent in rock and ice-climbing skills – although fitness and skill clearly played a part – but those who most passionately wanted to climb the mountain. It was written in their faces and in every move they made. Desire was the driving force.

In a way it was a surprise to me that I, too, developed this keen desire to climb Everest, for until this point I had rather wandered through life, expressing very little conviction for anything. Decisions at various crossroads of my life had been made on the basis of what I *should* do, or even what other people felt I should do, in order to give me what might be perceived as the best opportunities in life.

But Everest was different. There were no 'shoulds' about Everest. Quite the contrary; at the outset the whole venture looked professionally suicidal and for my health and safety, ill-advised. But it was something that had totally captured my imagination. To climb it was a want that bubbled up from within me, an intrinsic want. It was nothing that was put upon me by an external force.

We forget sometimes, but it is an authentic wish to do something, different for every individual, that energizes and inspires us. We love it, thus we do it.

It is often said that to have a vision – to be able to define clearly what it is we want to achieve – is all-important if we want success. This is true. But it is my belief that we need a very special sort of vision if we want to enjoy the journey on the road to achievement and perform absolutely to our best. We need a vision that is aligned to our intrinsic wants.

Defining the Dream 2

When Soichiro Honda developed his first truly commercial motorbike, a modest two-stroke model, he and his colleagues were celebrating the birth of the still unnamed machine. 'It's a dream!' said the wildly happy inventor. 'The Dream' promptly became the bike's name. Everybody has day-dreams of success and glory, and everybody has had moments, however small and fleeting, of dream realization.

But most people can also recall times when, if only they had backed their own instinct and judgement, they could have entered a future bonanza on the ground floor. Take the world's best-selling toys. Most of them were not so much invented as discovered, by men who noticed non-commercial phenomena (like children playing happily with pencils and empty thread spools) and dreamt up a related product that would sell in the millions. All the discoverers asked themselves the same question: Why wouldn't other children share the same pleasure?

Defining the dream always starts with an explicit or implicit 'Why?' The section above shows that Rebecca's Why? on her initial journey to Everest was natural for a journalist. Why do climbers climb? It seemed logical to try a little climbing to find the answer. A walk to the Advanced Base Camp at 6,450m (21,160ft) wasn't enough to fulfil the need. So she set herself to make a real climb, taking her to Camp 1. Getting to 7,125m (23,380ft) was a gruelling physical and mental test.

But there, as she writes so vividly, she found her answer. Knowing now why climbers climbed, she had also found her own dream: to come back to Everest and reach its (and her) summit. You don't have to wait for an epiphany to define the dream. Answering some straightforward questions about yourself and the organization in which you work establishes what you and your colleagues can do and truly want to do – with a passion.

Rebecca's dream and mine had a starting point in common. We were both connected with the *Financial Times*, though in very different eras. The paper sent her to the Base Camp on Everest from which she literally and metaphorically began her ascent. And the *FT* sent me to New York, as its one and only correspondent in the whole, staggering, gigantic United States of America.

At that point the US was staggering in more senses than one. President Eisenhower's highly conservative economics team had engineered an uncomfortable recession. Not that I was a great authority on such matters. I knew nothing of economics save what I had digested of Paul Samuelson's monumental tome – read while crossing in luxury on the Dutch liner, *SS Statendam*. So long as the *FT* was paying for this sybaritic First Class travel, I thought I should do some work on its behalf.

True, the great Samuelson didn't empower me to interpret the bear market then bothering Wall Street. But I was very soon to learn that nobody was so empowered. Thus, when the market rallied, the pundits explained the rise by hopes that a worsening Cold War would stimulate defence spending. Fine. When the market shortly thereafter suffered a relapse, though, the pundits were ready with an explanation; more or less the same one. The worsening Cold War, it was now feared, would become Hot – and real wars are bad for business.

I asked myself that great three-letter word: Why? Why were the pundits self-evidently wrong? And I realized, a neophyte on Wall Street, but a willing student of American capitalism, that writing about current events was no different from the historical studies which had delighted me at Christ's Hospital and Jesus College, Cambridge. When interpreting history, clever people, even the most eminent historians, saw what they wanted to see, not what actually was – whatever that might be.

Historical truths are not absolute entities. Today's truth is often tomorrow's falsehood, and vice versa. This discovery was little use in my first three years on the *FT*. Writing about such matters as the output of iron castings left little room for interpretation, and even when I graduated to larger matters, like iron and steel production itself, the *FT*'s approach to its subject matter was then too constipated to excite anyone – certainly not me.

I wanted above all to *write*. Writing seemed to me, as it does still, a summit of the human mind. What climbing became to Rebecca, writing had been for me from the beginning of my remembered time. But what should I write? At school and university, in addition to work, I had poured forth poems, short stories, satires, reviews, even a gossip column – shared with the future film and stage writer Stanley Price, a side-splitting humorist. Our piece of weekly juvenilia was published in *Varsity*, the student newspaper, and in hindsight both the column and my previous editing of the school magazine pointed in the same direction; journalism.

My ability must have been greater than I thought, for I was only 26 when Sir Gordon Newton, an editor of deserved renown, sent me to New York. Everything that followed had this as starting point. The US dominated the world of business as mightily as, in the early twenty-first century, it loomed, the sole superpower, over the geopolitical stage. Both dominions, it turned out, were built on shakier foundations than initially appeared. But history had taught me that even the greatest power always has limits, and that efforts to transcend those limits are always (and inevitably) self-defeating.

Peter M. Senge, a star professor at MIT, found the same phenomenon in companies which sought to exceed 'the limits to growth'. As he wrote: 'No matter how hard you push, the system pushes back harder'. That pregnant sentence lay far in the future in 1968 when the *Statendam* deposited me on the New York waterfront. I was soon trying to make journalistic sense of the large events that unfolded around me, including above all the epic struggle between Good and Evil, symbolized respectively by John F. Kennedy and Richard M. Nixon.

Rarely had black seemed blacker or white whiter – but that, of course, proved to be self-deception when the truth about Kennedy's political impotence and over-exercised sexual potency became clear. Just as history teaches, things are never what they seem to be. And that included the supremacy of American business. It was founded, so the story ran, on the superiority of American management, sustained by marvellous business schools; honed by the ruthless cut-and-thrust of commercial competition; conducted within a political system whose checks and balances automatically combined freedom and firm government, liberty and the rule of law.

There was some truth in this laudatory verdict, but also illusion and delusion. Much of the apparent strength of US business was not based on superior management, and still less on vibrant competition. With huge, protected shares of the largest market in the world, US companies had little to fear. There was no incentive to improve management practices that were sloppy and ineffective (as the Japanese were to prove). And, as President Eisenhower amazingly warned in his valedictory address, the military-industrial complex held the great democracy in a thoroughly undemocratic grasp.

Returning to the *FT* home base after three years, I had no opportunity to build on these perceptions. I ran a gossip column again (but this time for real, not for undergraduate fun). *Men and Matters* made me a kind of licensed jester in London. The paper's style and content had lightened up most remarkably in my absence, and the *FT*, with its richly talented staff, was now in the mainstream of Fleet Street. After two years on the column, though, I thought it time for me to go – and so, fortunately, did the *Observer*.

This was my spiritual home, as for all *soi-disant* right-thinking liberal intellectuals. I was wanted to edit what other papers called the City pages. The word 'City' stuck in the *Observer*'s politically correct throat, but the unit trust advertising was too large and valuable to forgo: so the section was labelled Business (as it still is). The *Observer*'s strategic need was obvious: producing authoritative coverage of business, financial and economic affairs to convince advertisers that the newspaper took the City seriously.

In some ways, I was the wrong person for the job. I had never covered the City, except peripherally; had few contacts; and had not the faintest idea what to do. In desperation, I turned to what I *could* do – write feature articles and personalized diary pieces – and married the twain. Thus I gave birth (anyway, so I claim) to the personalized coverage of these affairs that rapidly became the norm. It clicked, and so did my career.

Its development coincided happily with a great surge in business journalism and its revenues. One sector, though, lagged behind. Britain lacked a monthly business magazine with the glossy authority of Henry Luce's heavyweight *Fortune*. The gap had long tempted UK publishers. Anybody falling for that temptation was likely to consider me for editor: I had American experience, and both the gossip column and the *Observer* business pages had required editorial skills. When the call came, I was receptive. I wanted a wider role on the *Observer*, and played one at times; but wearing my City clothes, I felt an outsider in a paper which David Astor controlled with avuncular charm, and a sometimes infuriating mixture of charisma, professional skill, caprice and diffidence.

My call came from an unexpected source. I published a piece about how Haymarket, a tiny outfit, had snaffled a contract to publish the British Institute of Management's monthly from under the nose of Lord Thomson – the Canadian newspaper magnate who owned *The Times* and *Sunday Times*. My contact at Haymarket, the late Clive Labovitch, was known to me through mutual friends, but I had yet to meet his partner,

Michael Heseltine. I turned down Clive's first offer of the editorship, even though the *FT* and *The Economist* were Haymarket's partners. But then I seduced myself by the attractions of escape from the *Observer*'s habitual indecisions into a world under my own control.

Friends thought this a risky move. But as Rebecca's account of her first climb shows, you can't hope to ascend without risk. With powerful partners in the background, my long-term future was probably secure, anyway. And there was one risk that every career climber has to take – the risk that you will fail in the ascent. Sure, as Dirty Harry says, 'a man has to know his limitations'. Put more positively, you have to know how good you really are. Since there's only one way to find out, you must accept the next challenge and learn that crucial answer.

My main problem, again, was ignorance; I knew nothing about magazines and their production. But Labovitch and Heseltine had won considerable *succès-d'estime* with *Town* magazine, whose photography and design had revolutionized the glossies (but not their own then shaky finances). Once more, I married two disparate halves – combining the words of serious business pages with the visuals of a trendy fashion magazine. The positioning was easy. If American managers liked *Fortune*, I argued, then British managers probably would as well. However, the link with the BIM meant that *Management Today* (not a title I ever loved) contained more management material than its US model.

In April 1966, my baby was born. It was stuffed with ads (some sold personally by the irresistibly charming Garrett Drogheda, boss of the *FT*); replete with long and penetrating company profiles; and full of minor faults. I was brooding about these, walking down the corridor, when I passed a flushed and excited Heseltine. 'I've just realized', he said, 'that we've produced one of the world's most important magazines'. Admirably long-sighted, Michael had reached his Advanced Base Camp, from which further peaks could be scaled. And he had famously set those personal sights on the highest political peak of all.

As for me, *Management Today* launched a personal crusade. Overpraised American management might be, but it was better than British. We wanted to help British managers onwards and upwards, rising past the excuses (the politicians, the City, the unions) to create companies of real international strength. We wanted public services to follow the same path. The magazine's mood was hopeful, radical, investigative and activist. We gave detailed accounts of how the few exceptional top managers – like the late Lord Weinstock, the iconoclastic genius of GEC – ran their empires.

I found myself fighting this war against mediocrity on two fronts. The *Observer* had asked me to contribute a weekly column. Called 'Management in Action', the column attracted a following so loyal that it had a long, ghostly after-life of imagined appearances. In a sense, these columns did live on. They were the foundation of my first book, published at the beginning of the seventies as *The Naked Manager*. As the title indicates, the book was a debunking exercise. Descended from a family line of sceptics, I found debunking natural – and the cult of scientific management was a sitting target.

Imported from the US (of course), the cult held that managers trained in all the latest techniques at the best business schools could turn their talents to any businesses, and many of them at the same time. Hence the conglomerate, immortalized by Mel Brooks as *Engulf and Devour*, and doomed to failure. It was easy to demolish the myth, harder to argue the case for a rational, humane and honest management that combined realism with ideals. I ended up, somewhat to my surprise, singing the praises of Quaker businessmen for coming far nearer than most to this paradigm.

The positive message was probably obscured by the debunking. My reputation became that of a fierce critic, scourge of the bad, not (as I fondly thought) a kindly, generous defender of the good. But in truth my eyes remained fixed on the climb of my dream – leading managers in general, and British ones in particular, away from fixed ideas, changing fads and lazy habits and upwards to their own new heights. *The Naked Manager*, whose title passed into the language, was a best-seller in Britain, attracted a large advance in the US, and was translated into several tongues. But it was not my Everest: more my Kilimanjaro, a challenging walk on familiar journalistic terrain.

It was a breakthrough, though. As recommended elsewhere in this book, I took the opportunity as a foundation for other opportunities, writing books (over 50 by 2004) on many aspects of management, challenging the alleged supremacy of the US, pointing to the egregious follies of bankers (none of whom showed any interest in my findings), and returning always to the theme of *The Naked Manager* – that managers were and are far more capable than their records suggest, and far less wonderful than their self-publicity declares. They know what to do, they know how to do it, but their failure to do it often leaves them stuck at Base Camp.

That triplet ('They know what to do' … etc.) isn't mine. It's one of the pearls of wisdom scattered so liberally by Peter Drucker. From the first issue of *Management Today*, to which he contributed, he was my guide, a model to whose eminence I could only aspire. He had founded the modern literature of management, which his teaching has affected profoundly. He long ago planted the flag on the summit, and all other management climbers, in one way or another, are in his debt. Working as his chairman at several conferences was an intellectual and personal delight.

Speaking to general and in-house audiences was another path on my chosen ascent. I particularly needed the human contact after I withdrew from magazine publishing and thus from the daily association with others that is pleasure, stimulus and challenge rolled into one. From that base in *Management Today*, I had accompanied Michael Heseltine and Haymarket to their further summits: one by one, they conquered advertising (*Campaign*), accounting (*Accountancy Age*), computery (*Computing*) and so on. I was the Sherpa Tenzing to these expeditions, picking the route to each new audience and finding journalists who could help turn each new dream into reality.

There were other sectors than business – medicine, for example, and cars – in which Haymarket became market leader, and where I played some part. All in all, I learnt as much about management from Haymarket's ups and downs as from observing major companies, interviewing their bosses, editing *Management Today*'s articles, and reading books by other authors. Nothing beats being on the rock face. You learn from success, and you learn (probably more) from failure, in real time, with real results.

You can't understand macro-management, in other words, without mastering micro-management. Here, my major exercise was a series of small books most cleverly devised by Dorling Kindersley and named *Essential Managers*. Writing mini-encyclopaedias on everything from selling to strategy brought sales in many languages and many hundreds of thousands of copies. It reminded me, if reminding was needed, that out there in companies are individuals of many and varied talents and skills; and it is they, not the super-bosses in the headlines, who largely determine the fates of organizations.

This view was reinforced by consultancy work with an old Cambridge friend, the talented and patient Peter Zentner. Our analysis of the Halifax, in particular, showed how even the best of companies, being managed top-down rather than bottom-up, allow avoidable, obvious weaknesses to offset their strengths and frustrate their opportunities. Only in Japan could I find a different and far more productive philosophy and practice. True to form, though, most western managements either dismissed Japan's potent lessons or tried partial, inadequate imitations. Trying to influence the west with eastern ideas became another of my causes.

So did a prolonged effort to persuade western management that 'the Internet changes everything'. In two books, *Culture Shock* and *Riding the Revolution* (the latter written with Paul Spenley), I tried to get managements to understand the universal power of the new technology. Fortunately for them, the pressures of the digital revolution are so strong that everybody, willy-nilly, is now being pushed up the slope. Those who resist the shove will never reach the top; and there's no resting-place on the bottom.

Experience augmented and modified my views on management, but didn't alter their main thrust. On leaving magazines, I found new allies in this lifelong pursuit of the thinking manager, the one kind that can hope to succeed in fast-moving times. I formed a partnership with Edward de Bono, the great pioneer of lateral thinking, to write and publish our *Letter to Thinking Managers*. On my own, I wrote *The Fusion Manager*, which offers a new theoretical framework to replace the western delusion that there's 'One Right Idea' – which often includes the latest unsafe cult (like those of the omnipotent 'chief executive' and 'shareholder value').

With nonsenses like that still in wide circulation, I make no excuses for staying on the attack. There's all too much debunking that needs doing. Since *The Naked Manager* appeared, too many towering peaks of capitalism have been brought low, and too many idols of capitalism have developed lower limbs (and whole torsos) of clay, for the book's lessons to be thought redundant. Far from it. But that's a sad reflection. Is peak managerial performance as far away as ever?

In fact, British management has certainly improved. In the early summer of 2004 I visited three small-to-middling companies, thanks to the East of England Development Association, whose levels of basic efficiency, ambition, entrepreneurship, creativity and constructive human relationships would not have been much found in 1970 – or 1980 and 1990, for that matter. The trio designed microprocessors (ARM), brewed beer (Charles Wells) and tested racehorses for drugs (HFL). In these very different businesses, their philosophies and practices all drew successfully from the enormous amount of management lore built up over the past three decades.

Yet those three cheering visits coincided with the scandal of overstated oil reserves at Royal Dutch/Shell and the relapse of Marks & Spencer into struggling disrepair. Both had been stars in early issues of *Management Today*. From the perspective of 1966, their later troubles were unthinkable. From the viewpoint of 2004, the disasters were simply evidence that, in a world of unrelenting pressures, just as nothing succeeds like success, nothing fails like failure. Once give up striving for those summits, and you lose your foothold on the lower slopes.

Management is not eternal, like the mountains, but it does have eternal verities, and I love preaching and teaching those truths. Seize your opportunities. Develop your skills and those of others. Work in true teams. Lead and help others to lead. Find and nurture talent. Compete to win. Never let up. These verities are easy to write and hard to achieve – especially since you dare not neglect any one of the seven. Together they lead inexorably to your own summit.

Seizing the Opportunity 1

KILIMANJARO, 5,895M (19,340FT)

Kilimanjaro is a dormant volcano – one of the best known in the world, in part because of Hemingway's famous story of a dying writer, The Snows of Kilimanjaro. *In Swahili, Kilima Njaro means 'the mountain that glitters' and its snow-capped summit is an instant symbol of East Africa. It lies 250 miles south of the equator, just inside Tanzania's border with Kenya. A quick glance at the map reveals a* 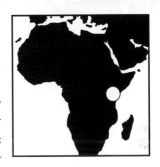 *curious kink encircling the mountain in an otherwise ruler-straight boundary between the two countries, explained by the fact that, in 1886, Queen Victoria gave the mountain to her German grandson Wilhelm as a birthday present. The mountain is surrounded by the hot, dry plains of the Masai steppe and known for its widely contrasting vegetation. Of the Seven Summits, it is the easiest to climb.*

Kilimanjaro was the first of my Seven Summits, not that I knew it at the time. On the return from my assignment in the Himalayas my sedentary life took on a rather more active turn. I was still working for the magazine, still based in London. But on a Friday evening I would run for the Llandudno train and scramble up a peak or two in

Snowdonia, before returning to the office with a rucksack chock-full of filthy kit on a Monday morning.

My holidays, too, were exclusively in the mountains – in Scotland, the Alps, Africa. In a couple of years I had managed – with the help of some professional guidance – to haul myself up Mont Blanc and the Ice Window route on Mount Kenya. So when a friend called me to seek suggestions on what she might do while on holiday in East Africa, it was perhaps no surprise that I answered, unreservedly, 'Climb Kilimanjaro. Can I come too?'

I had known my friend Lucy for the best part of a decade. We met on the platform of Farringdon tube station, both new to London, both a little lost in the metropolis, and both, it turned out, working as trainee journalists in the same building on the Goswell Road (so *that's* where I recognize you from!). Lucy went on to work for virtually every arm of the media and to travel extensively, but never to climb. And her inexperience as a climber, and climbing companion, was to be the major difference for me on Kilimanjaro compared with previous peaks. On Mont Blanc and Mount Kenya I was climbing with mountain guides. I took actions as instructed and left the planning and decision-making to others. On Kilimanjaro, I was to grasp the challenge myself.

Having said that, our trip to Kilimanjaro was a gentle introduction to expeditioning. Kilimanjaro might be the highest mountain on the African continent, but it can in no way be described as a technically arduous climb. There are tricky features on the mountain, such as the Breach Wall and the jagged spire of Mawenzi that pioneering climbers have sought and scaled. But essentially it is an oversized mound with gentle slopes running down to the sun-bleached plains of the Masai steppe. From a distance its shape resembles that of a pudding, and whether you climb it from the north, south, east or west, you can be sure of a footpath to the summit. Kilimanjaro is a high altitude walk, and by far the easiest of the Seven Summits.

It is also extremely regimented. The whole mountain experience is wrapped up by the Tanzanian government. Climbers pay a permit fee to enter the gate, and for each party it is obligatory to employ a local guide and porters. Tents, sleeping bags and food are usually thrown in, and for those opting for the well-trodden tourist trail there is bunked accommodation to boot.

But we wanted none of that. We had been strongly advised not to take the tourist route – the 'Coca-Cola route', it's called – unless, that is, we wanted to walk with hordes of people. The tourist route also has the disadvantage that trekkers are encouraged to climb it – up and down – in only five days, which for most of us simply isn't sufficient time to acclimatize.

Poring over maps we opted instead for the Machame route, which curls around from the south and which, little climbed then, would offer some degree of solitude. A little more circuitous than the Coca-Cola route, it would also take an extra day or two and give us more time to acclimatize.

As for the obligatory guide and the porters, we would go with them. But we would provide our own camping equipment and food, in an effort – artificial, I'll admit – to be self-reliant as far as possible.

I spent hours on the telephone to Lucy, reading out lists, checking lists, striking things off lists as much as adding things on, in order to all-importantly minimize the loads we were to carry. Equipment and clothing we would carry from home; food and fuel for our MSR stove we would buy locally. It was in Nairobi, I recall, before jumping on the bus across the border to Arusha, and then Kilimanjaro, that we wheeled a trolley around a supermarket to stock up for the climb ahead. I threw tens of chocolate bars into the trolley as fast as Lucy whisked them out again. 'You *will* want these,' I insisted. The fuel for the stoves we left until we arrived in Moshi, a small market town at the southern foot of the mountain. Fuel in Tanzania is notoriously contaminated and I spent the best part of an afternoon sitting in the garden of our guesthouse, filtering it from one can to another through coffee filter papers. Finally, we were, as far as it was possible, prepared.

Ψ

I was looking forward to the climb. Kilimanjaro, as we know, is a populated mountain, the result of which is that much of the wildlife has been frightened away; a four-striped grass mouse was the sum total of my animal spotting. Yet the mountain retains a character of its own, and its unusual topography continues to fascinate. When Kilimanjaro was first discovered by missionary Johann Rebmann in 1848, the great and the good at home in England, in the person of one Desborough Cooley of the Royal Geographical Society, didn't believe his report that its summit was capped with snow. How could that be, on the equator?

It is, of course, a textbook illustration of the effects of altitude on temperature. To climb it, you walk first through banana plantations on the rich volcanic soils of its lower slopes, then through forest, then heath, then high desert, and, finally – when the extreme altitude results in temperatures plummeting below zero – onto a glacial summit. Parallels can be drawn with walking across the lines of latitude from the equator to the north or south geographical poles.

Our journey was almost without mishap. 'Poli, poli, sister', the guide gently chastised, 'slowly, slowly', mindful that it never pays to force the body's natural pace of acclimatization. Slowly we climbed the mountain's lower slopes, drinking excessive quantities of water and resting a good deal more than we had in years.

Only our stove let us down, or rather the fuel – still clearly far from free of grit and grime. The stove spat and spluttered and finally ended its days with a gasp of exasperation from me, and a humble acceptance of rice and beans cooked on the porters' open fire. They had seen it all before.

With the patience of angels they stood by and watched as we struggled in the thinning air on the upper slopes. It is the last day that is a killer, rising at midnight and climbing 'poli, poli' on the steep, grey slopes of scree on the mountain's summit cone. Small chance of speeding now. Here oxygen is in radically reduced supply. Every step is an effort – lungs gasping for air, feet slipping infuriatingly on loose scree. Poli, poli. Breathe deep. Regroup. Find a rhythm. 'Don't fight nature but gently find a way to work with it', I whispered to myself. This is the secret to conserving energy and making progress in the upper reaches of the atmosphere (and in life generally, should we but remember).

At last there was a hint of light in the expansive African sky and we found ourselves standing on Kilimanjaro's caldera rim, looking out at a plump rising sun and far, far below, a blanket of pearly grey cloud stretching to the horizon. A slow stroll around the crater rim and we were on Uhuru Peak, the mountain's highest point, taking in the view of two further summits poking their heads above the cloud. Far in the distance was Mount Kenya, a peak I had climbed the year before and, closer to hand, Meru, a volcanic peak that stands sentry to Arusha some 50 miles away. It felt great stamping our feet in the snow, high up there on the roof of Africa. 'We can climb that one now', declared Lucy, pointing in the direction of Arusha. And in the course of the next few days, we did. The mountaineering bug, it seems, shows clear signs of being contagious.

REFLECTIONS

There is a story of a Tibetan lama instructing his pupils: he has a large vase and in it he places some rocks, right up to its rim.

'Is it full?' he asks.

'Yes', answers one of the young pupils.

The lama then takes some pebbles and places them into the vessel, around the rocks.

'Is it full?' he asks again.

One of the young pupils is catching on. 'No,' he answers, 'now you can add some sand.'

The lama adds sand, and finally tops up the vase with water. 'What,' he says, 'can we learn from this exercise?'

'That however much we fit into a day,' answers one, 'we can always do more.'

'No,' says the lama. 'The lesson is to put the rocks in the vase first.'

Do the important things first! The lesson is as true for managing one's day as for running one's life. Get on with it! Don't be put off! How often do we hear people proclaiming that they would love to learn to paint, for example, or take a sabbatical? I've done it myself. And years later we're no more gifted at art and just as overworked.

It is important to acknowledge that even when the desire to achieve something burns bright, it can be difficult to take the first step. It may appear too arduous, too expensive, or too time-consuming in our hectic lives. In this event, I sometimes play the trick of fast-forwarding time in my mind's eye. I know that some people imagine how their own obituary might read, and that this spurs them on to achieve. But not me – I won't be around to enjoy that. I prefer to think of myself at the end of my life, at a grand old age, with my family all around me. In those final hours I want to feel that I have made absolutely the most of my life on Earth. I know that I will have made many mistakes; I've clocked up enough already. But I don't want to have to say, 'If only ... I wish I had done this, or that.' We don't regret the things we have done; we only regret things we wish we might have done but somehow never got around to doing. And with this in mind it becomes crucial to fill the vase with those rocks first. Think important things first, and act now.

Another important thing became apparent to me on Kilimanjaro. On the mountain I had time to reflect. There I was climbing it with my friend Lucy at the age of 29, but in fact I had been drawn to it at a much younger age, when, as a student, I had worked on a farm on the edge of the Rift Valley in Kenya. It was this spell in East Africa that had prompted Lucy to call me to seek suggestions of what she might do there herself, which, of course, led to us climbing the mountain. I recall from that first trip to Kenya, aged 20, looking out of the aeroplane window to see Kilimanjaro standing proud above the African plains and thinking, 'one day I would like to climb that.'

Things seemed to be falling into place for me. Even as a young child I had loved to holiday on Dartmoor, in Derbyshire and the Yorkshire Dales, landscapes with rocky outcrops, burbling streams with plump, sheep-grazed grassy banks, and undulating hills and tors. When I thought about it, not even my chance invitation to Everest had been entirely out of the blue. Roger Mear had thought to invite me because two years previously I had expressed an interest in accompanying his expedition to climb K2. I had read about it in a newspaper and thought it sounded a bit of an adventure.

So, Kilimanjaro was my first step towards Everest. It allowed me to say, 'I'm on my way'. But it was also a wonderful affirmation that the mountains were where I wanted to be. To climb Everest was no longer just a dream; it was inherently the right choice for the person I was discovering myself to be. Several years of exploring various avenues in life and I had a strong sense that I was returning home.

Seizing the Opportunity 2

Opportunism has a bad name. The dictionary defines the opportunist as somebody without settled principles (as if those are always such a good idea), and who reacts to the circumstances of the moment (as if any other course is sensible, or even possible). In truth, success is about making the best of your opportunities; about obeying the wisdom of Soyen Shaku, the first Zen teacher to visit America, who wrote: 'When an opportunity comes do not let it pass by, yet always think twice before acting'.

That may sound paradoxical, but it's a highly intelligent paradox. The two extremes of responding to opportunity metaphorically fit the swimmer better than the mountaineer. The cautious soul dips a toe in the water to test the temperature before immersion. The bold spirit dives in at the deep end. The first, timid approach risks falling behind braver challengers without necessarily getting a better (but certainly belated) start. The braver plunge, though, heavily increases the risks of being wrong, striking your head on the bottom – and drowning.

There is a third way: getting thrown into the water, which can combine the disadvantages of the other two. The best-advised approach follows the wisdom of the Zen master. It falls between the two extremes, combining their advantages as much as possible. You only go in deep enough to test yourself, with the risks carefully controlled. But you also have total belief in ultimate success, and you build for that success from the very start.

What's true for individuals is true for organizations – which are, after all, individuals writ large. Thus, when Compaq, a tiny Texan start-up, launched into the infant market for 'portable' PCs its founders installed systems and an advertising budget fit for a future world leader in all PCs – which the start-up eventually became. Think Big but Start Small is a conservative yet ambitious strategy for seizing the main chance.

In Rebecca's programme for the Seven Summits, the strategy translated into Think Everest, but Start Kilimanjaro. Africa's highest mountain is a straightforward climb – as she says, more of a walk, really. But managers and climbers alike need to start within their zones of known competence, testing and building technique and experience, preparing for the next, sterner stage even while enjoying that marvellous exhilaration of initial success – the excitement which cries 'I'm on my way!'

There's a neat fit here between the opportunistic individual and the organization. Ideally they go through a shared experience of exploiting and exploring latent abilities and know-how to establish initial success: and then building on that platform by spotting and seizing the further opportunities that always arise. Compaq's case illustrates the point; the initial business was confined to that nascent market in (hefty) portable computers – a textbook example of competing in a major area (personal computing) while avoiding all the major competitors (which in those days meant, overwhelmingly, IBM.)

Portables were a whole new segment, a 'niche market'. The phrase is comforting to established businesses, because a mere niche sounds too small to merit their attention. But as Peter Senge, author of the penetrating *The Fifth Discipline*, has demonstrated, many important firms have consequently perished. 'Never Ignore a Niche' could be engraved on their tombstones. The small competitor left to flourish safely in its 'mere' niche transforms itself into a ferocious predator, tearing the establishment's large market into pieces across the board.

Those who attack a yet-to-exist market are truly brave, but better advised than anybody going head-on against established giants, and thus choosing a hard, maybe impossible ascent. Lower down on a high range, however, you may make a pleasant enough fortune yourself, or share in a pleasing corporate success, by climbing a foothill or two. The supreme prizes are obviously found higher up. But the summit of summits is not the only worthwhile opportunity. The best height you can achieve is by tautological definition the highest you can or wish to climb – and this personal peak is the all-encompassing objective, for all people at all times and at all levels.

The number of opportunities always far exceeds the number of achievements. A mountaineer's possible climbs are already there, rooted in Planet Earth. Whether you recognize them or not, the business and personal opportunities within your known world are infinite, far exceeding the number within your immediate grasp. The shortfall only matters if you fail to find a single good opportunity. But you may only need just one. Superb success in business, as in most creative endeavour, generally comes from One Great Idea – as John D. Rockefeller I demonstrated in the 1860s.

The sharpest businessman in history, and very possibly the ablest manager, Rockefeller, unlike his fellow petroleum pioneers, didn't believe that the prime opportunity lay in the insanely volatile business of exploration and production. Rather, refining, transportation and distribution, efficiently controlling access to markets, were the seat of future absolute economic power – as the fledgling tycoon saw with relentless clarity in his 20s.

In modern times, another unflinching 20-year old, Bill Gates, saw that the gargantuan opportunity in personal computing lay not in the machines themselves, but in dominating the market for the programs that alone made the machines useful. By fastening a hammerlock on the software business, Gates achieved the same irresistible muscle that Rockefeller had exploited, with similar ruthlessness, a century before.

In both cases, as in all others of sustained achievement, the One Great Idea acts as a launching pad for many others. In Compaq's history, the next signal opportunity was taken with the impudent (and, many thought, imprudent) advance from portable computing to the desktop, the province of the mighty and majestic IBM. Sensibly, Compaq still stayed as far from the regal presence and as tactfully as possible. Unlike most of the swarming IBM clones (all benefiting from the universality of the Microsoft operating system), Compaq only undercut IBM by modest amounts.

Ψ

All worthwhile opportunities give you an identifiable, all-your-own advantage – what a great advertising man (Rosser Reeves of the Ted Bates agency) called the Unique Selling Proposition. Your USP – personal or business – can lie anywhere. In Compaq's example, engineering quality and dealers-only distribution were the differentiators, enough to win Compaq a modest share of IBM's desktop domain. Massive and fast-rising profits followed: the company resembled a bike racer travelling in the slipstream of the leader, matching IBM's pace, but with less effort.

So far, so good. The young and the adventurous have an immense advantage over the old and the cautious when it comes to seizing opportunities. That's why large companies are rarely entrepreneurial. But the old conservative firms, remember, were once led by young adventurers themselves. That's why companies desperately need, not just young and vigorous spirits, but managers who will give youth every chance to apply its vigour. It's also why the vital young should never stay in a brain-dead company. Their own opportunistic vitality won't last for ever, and they should gather its rosebuds while they may.

Compaq itself made two serious generic errors as its clever opportunism became cemented into 'settled principles'. First, it allowed the Japanese, led by Toshiba, to become the lords of the portable PC. The next best opportunity, in business as in life, is usually the one closest to hand. Compaq continued to make excellent portables, but the richest rewards in laptops went elsewhere. Never allow another climber to steal your natural path. To change metaphors, the Mafia never allows others to muscle in on Cosa Nostra. Properly defended, 'our thing' is an ever-present opportunity.

Second, by hitching its wagon to IBM, Compaq chose the wrong star. The leader began to falter fast in PCs before the onslaught of the price-cutting clones. Compaq was caught in the wake of that ignominious collapse. Fortunately for the company, it possessed an arch-opportunist, a corporate mentor who saved the day – chairman Ben Rosen, whose own business (venture capitalism) was solely concerned with identifying and financing opportunities and opportunists. As Rebecca found time and again on the mountains, mentors are marvellous. Everybody should have one.

Under Rosen's lead, Compaq's board rebelled, ousted the founding chief executive, Rod Canion, and tackled the clones head-on. Freed from slavery to the wrong corporate model, Compaq trebled its market share, usurped world leadership from IBM and demonstrated the power of a most potent lesson: that taken opportunities need continuous reappraisal, leading if necessary to radical renewal.

This strategic programme exactly echoes the Japanese combination of *kaizen* (continuous improvement) with *kaikaku* (radical change). A Japanese leader like Toshiba will never leave even a world-beating manufacturing process alone, challenged by the knowledge that, since significant improvement is always possible, it must always be pursued. Self-improving managers, like self-improving athletes, have exactly the same right idea. Whatever you're doing can always be done better.

A sustained series of small, seized opportunities adds up to large pay-offs. But the bumper reward, unsurprisingly, comes from the Great Leap Forward. That's why Japanese leaders are on constant watch for the 'strategic inflection point' – a phrase used by Andrew Grove, chairman of Intel, the microprocessor maestros, to identify the moment when decisive change turns strategic preconceptions upside down. Grove was thinking primarily of technology – in particular, the Japanese onslaught in memory chips that had driven Intel into financial loss and deadly peril. But the same phenomenon can attack anywhere. The name of the Everest game, for a mountaineering instance, was changed for all contenders when Tibet closed the northern approach to the still unclimbed summit.

In a changing world, it's tempting, but desperately unsafe, to assume that all's for the best in the best of all possible companies. Grove has painted a stark picture of what happens inside organizations as even a splendid business passes its peak. This trauma is commonly regarded as a blow of fate. Much more accurately, it is a lost opportunity. Strategic inflection points always create opportunities, which are rarely seized by incumbent market leaders – and for no good reason, just the bad one of complacency.

I saw the sadness of self-delusion at first hand after interviewing one of the happy band of founding brothers, all consequently multi-millionaires, who had created Compaq. How long could the existing strategy sustain the growth saga? After careful study, opined the former founder, management had concluded that the existing strategy was good for another ten years. Ten minutes would have been more like it. The company was just about to plunge into losses as its 'business model' was shattered by aggressive clones, led by another near-juvenile genius, and ace opportunist, Michael Dell.

Dell, with his direct sales (cutting out the middleman, making made-to-order machines, and streamlining production), was inventing the future. Compaq's Canion lost his job by defending a very recent past. The opportunist is always hoping to exploit the present and thus create the future. To turn that hope into actuality, you need only four attributes:

1   *Ability*. Do I have the basic skills, aptitudes and attitudes required to exploit this opportunity?

2   *Urgency*. Will I treat this opportunity as a life-or-death priority, with a driving, stretching schedule?

3   *Persistence*. If I'm succeeding, and also if I'm not, will I try, try again?

4   *Change*. Do I constantly watch for change in the business and its environment and change accordingly – at speed?

For Andy Grove's Intel, the new opportunity, to change from memories to microprocessors, popped up in the very nick of time. Fortunately, top management spotted what many, including its own marketers, failed to believe: that the future, not just of Intel but the entire digital revolution, rested on the new invention. Again, in hindsight, this was only common sense: a chip that could be programmed just like a computer surely had the world at its feet.

Ψ

As Edward de Bono has pointed out, creative breakthroughs always look obvious in hindsight. The same is true of successful opportunism. It was obvious that personal computers would find their way on to every desk and into most homes: but only a few people, led by the precocious Bill Gates, saw the obvious and acted on their vision – not in the sense of a dream, but in that of 20–20 eyesight.

Similarly, it's blindingly obvious that you shouldn't buy stocks and shares that are keenly sought and priced above their intrinsic value: you should surely do the opposite, seeking solely the opportunity to buy stocks which are demonstrably undervalued. Anybody can see that. But only Warren Buffett became the world's second richest man, after Gates, by capitalizing on the obvious with dedicated determination.

Both of these extreme and wonderful examples are cases of contrarianism – going against the crowd, a route that is always an abundant source of prime opportunities. The mob, though, believes that its common view is common sense. It was obvious to nearly everybody in the computer business that Ken Olsen, the hero of Digital Equipment, was right. Who on earth would have any use for a Gates-powered personal computer? But then, who in their right mind would, like Buffett, buy unwanted stocks and shares?

Doesn't the collective wisdom of the marketplace far outweigh the brainpower of a single investor? Isn't that just common sense? It turns out that common sense has two meanings. The first refers to propositions that are straightforward, logical, verifiable and verified, but may actually be uncommon (see Buffett, above). The second meaning refers to views that are very widely held (hence the 'common'), but may be both illogical and untested (hence not sense, but its absence).

If you study company portfolios, for example, you would conclude that hanging on to businesses and brands must be a strategy of enormous value. Thus, according to the *Harvard Business Review*, Diageo maintained 35 booze brands (for which read 'businesses') in 1999. Yet 27 of the 35 brands accounted for only half the group's sales and a mere 30% of profits. In 1996, Nestlé had over 8,000 active brands; only 2.5% contributed to profits. Procter & Gamble marketed more than 250 brands in 1992; between then and 2002, the top ten alone earned over half of the company's sales and profits and generated two-thirds of sales growth. In 1999, Unilever's brands totalled 1,600. It took three-quarters of them to produce 10% of profits. Yet all four of those portfolios actually offered a significant range of opportunities:

- You can develop profitable brands further by investment, innovation and aggressive management.

- You can return losing brands to profit by the same combination of positive, proactive policies.

- You can add further brands by new product development or purchase.

- You can sell brands, winning or losing, to a better home.

- You can simply withdraw brands from the market, and cut your losses.

- You can just soldier on with portfolios in which a small number of winners support (or are held back by) the much larger number of losers.

A moment's thought shows that the last of these is no opportunity at all. It merely continues, as most people do, with the status quo. Very often, people miss opportunities through fear – above all, fear of failure. They hesitate to leave the job they have, for example, because they fear they will fail in the new employment. They don't climb mountains because they fear they will fall. Fear is a bad master, and a tyrannical one. But why would fear drive a great company to persist with money-losing brands in markets rich with better opportunities?

The economic realities get outweighed by emotional forces almost as strong as fear. Every brand has a squadron of managers and a corps of other workers behind it. So deep is the commitment, including the hangover from historical success, that often only disaster, actual or incipient, forces people to abandon their loyal conservatism. They may then find and seize marvellous opportunities to recreate the company and even surpass its best former days – as at both Compaq and Intel.

Another excellent, conventional way of missing opportunities is that famous old advice about 'sticking to the knitting'. Since diversification into unfamiliar opportunities so rarely works, it seems sensible to browse only on your home turf. The trouble here is that this automatically and starkly limits your choice. In their private lives, people don't have to accept limitation to one class of opportunity. Why should organizations restrict themselves to a narrow field of opportunities when they house so many different kinds of people – and thus different sets of skills?

Anyway, after five years of study, Chris Zook and James Allen of the consultancy Bain & Co found that you really *can* have your cake and eat it. That means staying within your areas of competence and experience, but at the same time developing strong, new, profitable growth by the strategy most likely to succeed – pushing out the 'boundaries of the core business into ... adjacent space'. In other words, you stick to the spirit of the Zen teaching – careful opportunism – cited at the start of this section.

Moving into an entirely novel area, either by internal initiative or external acquisition, is inherently risky – which is, of course, why these strategies commonly fail. But what the two Bain authors call 'adjacencies' are what I have described elsewhere as 'concentric' expansion. That is, all the seized opportunities revolve around the central core, Microsoft being a stunning example: virtually all its wondrous growth revolves round the original breakthrough in PC operating systems.

Opportunity after opportunity has been seized from this base, from Office to Explorer and Outlook Express. Nike, cited by the Bain pair, is another example. Since 1987 it has vastly outgrown Reebok, then twice as big as Nike. After expanding sales 6.7 times, Nike now outsells its rival over fourfold. The opportunistic formula is to create a leading position in shoes in the chosen sports market; then widen into clothing for that market; next, step up from accessories to major equipment; and finally go global.

This formula is repeatable, and each successful repetition improves the odds on future success. Having your cake and eating it thus hinges on taking advantage of the opportunities that lie closest to hand – in the actual conduct of your business or your career. The Seven Summits opportunity was all the easier for Rebecca to seize because she had already climbed Kilimanjaro and Everest. Strategy formed and well-executed in this manner involves no pies in the sky.

Nor does taking advantage of 'negative opportunity'. Stopping a £100,000 loss is just as effective as making £100,000 on a positive venture – and probably much easier. Go back to those four great, brand-burdened companies. What created the hundreds of lost, loss-making brands in the first place? Somebody at Diageo, at Nestlé, at Procter & Gamble and at Unilever once saw every one of these products as a positive opportunity. The now-losing products may even have enjoyed long-term past success. What happened? How did a good opportunity deteriorate and become a lost cause?

The answer is inseparable from an attribute that plays an indispensable role in seeing and seizing opportunities – including the chance to climb the Seven Summits. That attribute is Ambition. Ask 100 owner-managers to plan an ambitious future for themselves, and you'll be lucky (as I have seen in practice) to find five prepared to demonstrate this admirable sense of purpose, this urge to achieve something truly worthy of their lives and their talents. Yet without ambition, your mind will not be set to spot either the right opportunity or the right people, ideas, chances, moments, or anything else that will help you on your achieving way.

At some point, people stop being ambitious for brands and businesses. In a self-fulfilling prophecy, the latter promptly join the living dead. I was once discussing such a brand, a lager. The top manager concerned had long since slashed its marketing support to nothing – so I asked him to give the brand away (to me, of course). 'Don't be stupid', he replied, 'It's worth millions!' It might as well have been worthless, since its latent riches, which lurk in any long-standing brand, were simply not being exploited.

What if the beer had belonged to Mr and Mrs Lager and their little family of boy and girl Lagers; would this malign neglect have been as likely? Surely a sentient bunch of Lagers would have striven with might and main to protect and enhance their inheritance – like the Bedford firm, Charles Wells. This became the largest of the few remaining private, family-owned brewers by seizing broad opportunities for new or improved products and processes within its narrow remit – that of making excellent and sought-after beers for carefully defined markets.

Think of yourself as a family business. You have assets, mental, emotional and physical. A whole world of opportunities surrounds you and your several talents. Which of those opportunities best match those assets? Which, above all, best promises to satisfy the ambitions that are closest to your dreams and your realities? The fit may never be perfect, but it can be wonderfully good. And it's tautologically certain that, if you don't look out for opportunities, you won't see them, and if you don't see them, you certainly won't take them. And that is no way to reach the tops of the mountains.

SUMMIT 1

- Think Everest, but start Kilimanjaro – or **think big**, but **start small**.

- Give **priority** to what is most **important**: 'put the rocks in the vase' before anything smaller.

- Remember that **desire** drives everything. Human beings veer towards that which gives them pleasure.

- Realize that even when the desire to achieve burns bright, the first step can be difficult; take it **without delay**.

- **Don't** let yourself end up **regretting** things you might have done, but somehow never got around to doing.

- Obey this: 'When an opportunity comes do not let it pass by, yet always **think twice** before acting'.

- Go in deep enough to test yourself, with risks carefully controlled, but with **total belief** in ultimate success.

- Stay within your areas of competence and experience, while **developing** strong, new, profitable, **concentric growth**.

- See **contrarianism** as an abundant potential source of prime opportunities: go against the crowd!

- **Set your mind** to spot the **right opportunities**, people, ideas, timing, etc. that mark the road to your ambitions.

Developing the Skills 1

DENALI, 6,194M (20,321FT)

The Native American name of Denali is now the accepted name for a peak once more commonly called McKinley. Denali means 'the high one' and indeed, as the highest peak in the Alaska Range, it rises abruptly from the Arctic tundra and offers one of the greatest vertical gains in the world: 6,000m from foot to summit. Lying just south of the Arctic Circle at 63° north, it is also reputedly one of the

coldest mountains in the world, and climbers have been known to 'flash-freeze' on its slopes. At the centre of a vast national park of the same name, Denali was originally named by gold prospectors after President William McKinley, who was shot dead in Buffalo, New York, by a Polish anarchist, Leon Czolgosz, in 1901.

It was in the year following Kilimanjaro that, eyes focused on Everest and keenly aware that I had a lot yet to learn, I set out as one of a party of twelve to climb Denali.

Plans for Everest were shaping up well by this time. For a while it had seemed such a bold ambition that I had hardly dare mention it to anybody, but as time ticked by I became immersed in the climbing world. I climbed on London climbing walls and

Snowdonian rock; I drank in climbers' pubs, and slowly I found confidence to express my ambition to those around me.

I can thank two people for securing my trip to Everest. The first was a new character in my life, a financier and keen rower and runner called Peter Earl, who, true to form as it turned out, went on a trekking holiday in the Himalayas and came home with a permit in his pocket to climb Mount Everest.

And the second was John Barry, a professional mountain guide who Peter approached to lead his Everest expedition, and who, by chance, had taught me all I knew about mountaineering. It was John who had led me up Mont Blanc and the Ice Window route on Mount Kenya. And it was John who was now to lead our group of twelve – the majority of us being booked to climb the South East Ridge of Everest the following year – on Denali.

We were a motley crew, some with a good deal of mountaineering experience and others, like me, with not so much at all. And Denali is a monster of a peak. At 6,194m (20,321ft), it stands head and shoulders above its neighbouring peaks in the Alaska Range and just a smidgen below the Arctic Circle. As noted, this combination of geographical features – high altitude and extreme northerly latitude – makes it reputedly one of the coldest mountains in the world. In John's view it would serve as an excellent training ground for Everest, both for us to climb together as a team, and, for those of us with less experience to pick up the requisite mountaineering skills.

It was the latter that caused me some anxiety. I was convinced then – as I am now – that the most important characteristic of any individual wanting to climb Everest is an overriding desire to do so. And this I had, in spades. But I also understood that desire is no substitute for the required skills. It is a prerequisite that fuels the energy to acquire the skills, and now my ability to learn them was going to be put to the test.

It was daunting. I had limited experience of climbing on snow and ice in the Alps but Denali was altogether on a different scale. It was much higher than the Alps and, we could assume, colder. We would be on the mountain for two, maybe three weeks; and for much of this time we would be on a glacier. There were rules surrounding rope work and glacial travel to learn about, and the intricacies of pulley systems, prussic knots and belays to execute crevasse rescues. Not to mention the domestics of stoves – temperamental at higher altitudes – and the pitching of tents in icy conditions.

The cold was a particular concern of mine. I'm not physically well-suited to this game. I suffer from Raynaud's disease and my fingers turn shades of purple and white on the mildest of winter days on London's streets. Would I lose my fingers and toes to frostbite? And would I be fit enough? Would I be able to keep pace with the rest of the team?

Ψ

My only consolation was the statistics. Denali – because it's the highest mountain in North America – draws hordes of climbers from gateways around the world, and of those who attempt to climb it, a good half fly home having stood on the summit. Not bad odds.

'Don't be fooled, though,' said Roger, whose expedition I had accompanied to Everest, and who, impressively, had scaled one of Denali's harder routes, the Cassin Ridge, in deepest winter. 'Denali isn't a mountain to be underestimated.'

These cautionary words resounded in my ears, in a snow hole. Of the twelve of us who had stood at the base camp at the start, four had peeled off to climb the Cassin Ridge, leaving the rest of us to climb the less challenging and more popular West Buttress; the 'dog run' it's called. We couldn't fail. Except that now we were stuck at some 4,330m (14,200ft) in a large snowy basin on Denali's western flank – unable to climb higher and unwilling to climb down – and forced by high winds to abandon our tents and burrow deep, like high altitude moles, underground. I shared a snow hole with four of our team, and there were three others in a cave dug deep in the snow next to ours. We were there for four days, maybe five. It's easy to forget.

One nameless, numberless day merged into another in an unstructured sort of timelessness in this northern land where, in May – the month we were there – darkness falls only a couple of hours in twenty-four. I suppose we could say we were comfortable, if a little cramped. Three of us lay prostrate on one side of a snowy shelf on which we cooked, two on the other. Over a period of a couple of days the ceiling sagged under its own weight and that of newly fallen snow so that sitting upright was made impossible. But we were warm, relatively so. The temperature hovered around –10° C; and most importantly we were protected from the storm. Snow is a good insulator and all that we could hear of the wind was an occasional rumble, like the sound of a distant tube train passing by.

Food supplies ran low. We ate pasta; no salt. And M&Ms. We chatted, played word games, told and re-told jokes until conversation ran dry. We read books, brewed countless cups of tea and tried, desperately, to sleep.

It was hard to sleep. At night snow continued to fall and drifted, blocking the entrance to our snow hole. No matter what we tried, still it drifted. We constructed protective walls of snow bricks, excavated troughs and tunnels, and come morning the entrance was still blocked with a thick caking of snow, every time. In an effort to keep an airflow we cut a small chimney through the roof, but this snowed over too, despite efforts to keep it clear with a protruding ski pole. What happens if one runs short of air? Does one awake? Or fall unknowingly into a coma? I wanted to know.

On occasions we were forced to venture outside, for sanity's sake, or to use the communal, extremely exposed long drop, dug in the middle of this icy wilderness by conscientious rangers in an attempt, successful in the main, to keep the mountain clean. We weren't alone at 4,330m (14,200ft). There were sixty climbers or so – Americans, Koreans, French, German, Swiss – all dug in, waiting.

The morning of the fourth day – or was it the fifth? – I woke early, my bladder wanting out. The boys were asleep. I scrambled out of my sleeping bag and pulled on my windproofs over layers of fleece – fleece I hadn't shed since I had set foot on the mountain. Boots, over-gaiters, gloves, hat, goggles, face-mask; I never left the snow hole with less. And a shovel.

Gathering my strength, I dived into the entrance chamber of the snow hole, which by now had been shaped and moulded into an impressive tunnel, narrow but about 6m in length. I was forced to lie on my belly, stabbing at the snow somewhere above my head and having no choice but to shovel the snow back around my body so that I was cocooned, unable to move.

Three times I retreated, and three times forced myself back, until, at last, I broke a window to the outside. And stopped. A storm blew fiercely. Spindrift swirled about me, masking my goggles and freezing my hands, and nothing in me could force my body through the tiny escape hole. I retreated, eyes welling with tears.

It got worse that day, or rather, sadder. It had only been a fortnight earlier that the twelve of us had landed in a small aircraft on Denali's lower slopes. The sun was shining and we were enthusiastic to embrace the challenge ahead. Now three of our friends in the neighbouring snow hole – Peter and Mike and Brian – who had been good enough to dig us out of our snow hole that morning, had bad news to report. The temperature outside, they said, was –38° C and the wind speed was in excess of 80mph. The wind had broken the anemometer. It was the worst weather recorded on the mountain in 30 years – my lifetime, damn it. And there were no signs of improvement. They, and Sandy, our doctor, too – who had been one of the number in our snow hole for the last few days – had pressing engagements at home and couldn't wait.

Ψ

It was a sad moment to see them go. John roped them up and sent them on their way. 'Just stood there, watching,' he said, 'until they disappeared out of sight.' We could only imagine them retracing our steps through the various camps to the landing strip at 2,100m (7,000ft). By morning they'd be on an aeroplane to Talkeetna, then

Anchorage and home. And they weren't alone. Of the sixty or so climbers that had been pinned in at 4,330m (14,200ft), a good number roped up and headed home.

Of our team, there were only four remaining now – John, two climbing friends, Dave Halton and Paul Deegan, and myself; and that afternoon, of course, the sun shone.

'Should have persuaded them to stay', muttered John. Maybe. Maybe they would have done.

It felt so good to be out of the snow hole, stretching our limbs and squinting all the while into the sun. The scene was brilliantly white and clean, and it was warm, the sun prickling our skin. Everyone enjoyed the same pleasures that afternoon, mingling and chatting away to one another, as if in a park on a Sunday afternoon.

But it was only a temporary reprieve. The following morning, Bob, an American, virtually spherical in his puffed-up down suit, fought his way though the storm and squeezed himself into our snow hole. 'Heard the news? A Swiss guy, a guide, died in camp last night. Cerebral oedema.' He went on: 'And that's not all. Two bodies have been found on the Cassin, and three Koreans fell just here, on the Orient Express. All dead.'

Six people. 'Do you know what that makes me think?' said John. 'This whole bloody game is a waste of time.'

But my mind was on the Cassin. Were they our guys, dead? 'It's not Bill and Harry, or Smiler, or Brian. They're just too experienced.' These were John's words, and his unquestioning faith was all we had to hold on to.

For the first time I had very serious doubts whether we would make it to the summit. Spirits were low. This mountain was a killer, and the winds continued to blow. We spent three more days in the snow hole ... and then the weather changed, for a day.

Just the motion of moving – upwards – pumped energy back into our bones. We travelled light now – just rucksacks, no sleds – up a 45 degree headwall onto the crest of the West Buttress; and for an hour or so the sun shone so fiercely that it seemed impossible that a storm could ever blow again. But the weather is a fickle thing, particularly at altitude. The mountain threw us its worse once again and any chance we had of climbing the length of the ridge to an inviting plateau at 5,200m (17,000ft) was thwarted.

Instead we pitched our tent short of the ridge on an exiguous, shark-fin crest. We had no choice, other than to go down. The temperature was worryingly low; the wind, in gusts, knocked us to our knees, and when finally we succeeded in pitching our tent, the poles buckled and the canvas ripped. I didn't sleep that night, uncomfortable in the knowledge that a tent, plus occupants, had been blown off this very spot. We discussed the idea of tethering a rope to harness around our waists, through the zippered door and around a rock, so that we, at least, should be secured to the mountain if the tent was ripped violently from its anchors. But shame to say we couldn't muster the strength to face the storm; so we stayed put, churning these worries over and over, for a second night, and a third.

We were tiring. Time was running short and already we had missed our return flight to London. If I held on a couple more days I would more than likely lose my job. Others had worries too.

What to do?

On the last possible day that we could afford to hold on and make a summit attempt, the wind dropped. The weather wasn't good, but it was fair. And we went for it.

Just over twelve hundred metres – from 4,938 m (16,200ft) to 6,194m (20,321ft) – is a lot to climb in a day, when the air is so thin; and we moved slowly, painfully so.

'What do you think?' asked Dave. We still had a good way to go and it was late, and bitterly cold. We dared not take off our gloves for fear of frostbite.

'I'm not turning back now,' said John.

'Nor I.'

At 9.00pm that evening we stood on the summit of Denali. The sky overhead was perfectly clear and the Alaska Range stretched before us, with light cloud filling the valleys thousands of feet below. Everything was tinged pink. And thankfully – it being the month of May – we had daylight enough to descend safely.

REFLECTIONS

The overriding lesson learned from Denali was just how serious a place the mountains are, and how devastating the consequences if things go wrong. Mountains can look so benign in the sunshine, and then, in a moment, metamorphose into a killing ground.

Thank God, John was right: it wasn't our friends who were killed on the Cassin Ridge. Nonetheless, young lives were lost, parents and loved ones left to grieve. I didn't need to suffer the loss of one of our own team to appreciate that death can be perilously close to hand, and that mountains must be approached with the utmost respect.

It was really this that dictated much else that I learned on Denali. I had approached the mountain anxious about a number of specific technical skills that I would have to learn, but discovered there was a further raft of things to consider. Climbing a mountain is a marathon; it isn't a sprint. What really counts is a conscientious ability to look after oneself every minute of every hour of every day. It's about eating, drinking and sleeping enough, in order to maintain strength in an environment that conspires, it seems, to make you sick.

And it isn't just mountain sickness a climber has to consider. At high altitudes the UV light is of such intensity that neglecting to wear sunglasses, even for a matter of minutes, can result in snow blindness. It is so cold that exposed skin can be frostbitten in seconds. So climbers must laboriously dedicate hours to melting snow and preparing drinks; to eat, even when nausea makes them retch; to shield their eyes with goggles, even when they're frosted over in whirling snow; and, of course, to protect extremities from the extreme cold and make sure – whatever happens, make sure – that their core body temperatures are never allowed to fall.

The good news is that none of these things is complicated. It just requires unwavering attention to detail, as do most things in life if they are to be done well. Reassuringly, to be diligent and pay attention to detail is within all our capabilities.

However, it would be ignorant of me not to be acutely aware of the sensitivity of this subject. It is true that diligence greatly increases the chances of success and reduces the physical risks of climbing a mountain. But it does not eliminate risk. People still die.

I once heard a friend – a mountain guide – say that all accidents in the mountains are the fault of the climber. And in a sense he is right. But it seems to me a harsh judgement. Of course mountaineers are fallible and prone to errors of judgement. Some will knowingly push the limits, driven by a pioneering spirit to break new ground. But even the most cautious climber might be unlucky and be caught in a freak avalanche or sérac fall. Or to fall victim to cerebral oedema, like the Swiss guide at our camp at 4,330m (14,200ft). He was a man, surely, who must have been experienced at such altitudes.

Take this argument to the extreme and the only way to reduce risk altogether – assuming this is one's objective – is to not venture to the mountains at all.

If we are to look at this in a wider context, is this an alternative? Are we not to take on any challenges in life? The risks in our domestic lives and in the world of work may be manifested in different forms. It is rare that we risk our lives but we might nonetheless risk our livelihoods, or bankruptcy, or simply failure to achieve what we set out to do. But is this to stop us progressing? I think not – because to stagnate is far the worse option. For individuals, stagnation is a sort of spiritual death, and for companies, stagnation is suicide, for sure as the light of day, competitors will continue to innovate aggressively. Far better then to move forward, develop a keen awareness of the risks, and mitigate them as far as is possible.

Moving on, if there was one consolatory lesson learned on Denali it was that the technical skills that I had been so concerned about – glacial travel, crevasse rescue and so on – proved less daunting, more straightforward than I had expected. It turned out, as is so often the case, that the fear was far worse than the reality. They required practice, of course, but with time and training I began to feel that they were within my grasp.

The lesson here is not to be fearful of undertaking something that might seem baffling or incomprehensible, but to trust that we will find a way, and that with time and training the requisite skills to achieve our goals can be acquired.

Another key lesson was the importance of planning and preparation. This might seem an obvious requirement but it struck me with full force when, after several days in a snow hole, a number of climbers roped up and headed for home. Many did so simply because they ran out of food, or fuel to melt snow for drinking water. It was then that I was enormously thankful that we had an experienced leader who had considered every eventuality, even before we had left home. I don't suppose he expected that we would be hit by such diabolical weather, but he had at least thought about it and reasoned that it was within the realms of possibility, and catered accordingly. Without his careful contingency planning, we never would have had supplies sufficient to make it to the top.

It's a stark truth, but those who succeeded in climbing Denali that year weren't the toughest, or the fittest, or the most accomplished climbers. They were those who simply asked, 'What if ...?' 'What if we are held up in bad weather?', and who had bothered to bring along a little extra food and fuel, just in case. Thorough planning and preparation are essential if success isn't to be left to chance.

There was a lot I learned on Denali, not least of which was the method by which I learned what I did. It may have been uncomfortable at times but it was crucial, if I was to learn, that I was physically *on* a big mountain, that I was personally able to experience the plummeting temperatures and the violence of the storms. None of this could I have learned from a book. There's no doubt about it: if something is to be understood, it is to be experienced. So-called 'experiential learning' is the most effective and powerful learning there is.

Lastly, Denali afforded me confidence. I knew from this very real and practical experience that I could climb to 6,194m in extreme northerly latitudes – equivalent, say, to 7,000m in the Himalayas (due to a geographical phenomenon that means the atmosphere is heavier on the equator than at the poles). Maybe, I thought – just maybe I could climb the highest mountain in the world. Why not?

Developing the Skills 2

The late Mark McCormack had it right. As the title of his bestseller insisted, there are things they 'don't teach you at Harvard Business School'. But education can teach you *how* to learn the unteachable; and that is essential. Just like Rebecca on Denali, at every stage in a managerial career, the climber needs to master new knowledge and know-how. Great learning won't create a great manager. But it provides the tools, the intellectual foundations of managerial greatness.

If you want to progress from Kilimanjaro to Everest, you had best learn about glacial travel, rope work, sheltering in extreme conditions – and, most important of all, about yourself. How good am I? That's the crucial, unavoidable question. That's what tests the key areas of managerial competence, including self-appraisal, and what shows how you can cope when the going gets rough and tough – as it surely will.

For Rebecca, the moments of that truth came on the highest peak in North America, and reputedly the coldest in the world. The mountain duly greeted her with severe storms and the iciest conditions in 30 years. Managers can expect analogous tests at least once in their careers. Like many Denali climbers that year, many managers give up in crisis situations. Others can be inspired by the fact that Rebecca and three companions made it to the top – after days and nights pinned down by the diabolical, deadly weather.

Adversity is the keenest test of human capacity, not least in management. That's why so many heroes – like Jack Welch of General Electric or Sir John Harvey-Jones of ICI – revealed their true ability by turning other people's failures into their own successes. The skills required by turnaround managers are exactly the same as those of management in general. And those skills can all be learnt.

I am not referring here to the specific skills required in everything from organizing to communicating, decision-making to motivating, interviewing to negotiating, and so on and on. When writing ten ultra-compact volumes on such subjects for the *Essential Managers* series, I was impressed by the endless range of skills required of today's managers. Equally impressive, the demands are matched by an extraordinary breadth and depth of knowledge about how these skills can be developed and applied – in a word, learnt.

It's your duty as a manager – not least, your duty to yourself – to ensure that you acquire these skill-sets as needed, and that you keep your armoury in state-of-the-art condition as the years go by. It's also your duty to see that those for whom you are responsible do likewise. That will determine their personal success – and therefore that of the organization. In this age, how people are selected, developed, deployed and motivated decides competitive strength and comparative performance far more than anything else.

But the essential skills of management go far beyond marketing techniques and budgetary know-how. How do you rate on these Eight Elements of behaviour?

1   Do you always have a purpose – asking, 'what needs to be done?'

2   Do you ask, and do, 'what is right for the enterprise' – and not just for interest groups within and around the enterprise?

3   Do you develop and execute action plans?

4   Do you take responsibility for decisions?

5   Do you take responsibility for communicating?

6   Do you focus on opportunities rather than problems?

7   Do you know how to run productive meetings – and actually do it?

8   Do you think and say 'we' rather than 'I'?

There really should be a further question. If you can't answer YES eight times, will you promptly set about mastering the missing skills? The questions are derived from the highest possible authority, Peter Drucker, greatest of gurus, and from the highest possible sources – the best CEOs he has observed in 60 years of close personal attention. Writing a lead article in the *Harvard Business Review*, Drucker dismissed the widely held idea that personality type determines the success of business leaders. He has found high-achieving CEOs in extroverts and in near-recluses, in easy-going *laissez-faire* fellows and in control freaks, in the generous and in the mingy.

But those Eight Elements are universal among the elite of management – and a glance will show that they are all teachable. The indispensable teacher, of course, is yourself. In my experience, the best people in any field, not only business, are determined, often fanatical self-improvers. You may be a world-beating goal kicker like Jonny Wilkinson, but you devote long hours every day to the practice that makes you perfect. And if performance slips from your self-imposed highest standards, you go back to the practice pitch.

The self-development is central. But you wouldn't want to rely on self-help when planning to assault any of the Seven Summits (with the possible but doubtful exception of Kilimanjaro). Like Rebecca, you would seek the best mentors, guides and coaches. You may find the help you need in business education, in its many and varied manifestations: it may be provided by senior colleagues: but even the greatest pros in sport and the arts – people whose own advice is itself much sought after – will depend on expert advisers.

The presence (or absence) of the latter doesn't end the story. Book learning and article education have a significant role. The key weapon of management at all levels is The Idea. I wrote truly long ago that I've never opened a book on management, or an article for that matter, which didn't contain at least one useful, stimulating, insightful or thoughtful idea. Sometimes whole careers, entire enterprises, can be inspired by one book.

The most admirable of the privately-owned food manufacturers, Mars, was built by the wholly remarkable Forrest Mars partly on the ideas, read in a book, of an otherwise obscure British economist. Naturally, this thinker isn't the person who deserves the credit. That belongs to the American entrepreneur who not only imbibed the wisdom, but turned it into effective action. That's Drucker's fifth Element of super-boss behaviour. He or she draws up action plans – and turns plans into irresistible deeds.

Management is above all a matter of behaviour, as Drucker discovered from those sixty years of studying CEOs. It's not just your own behaviour that benefits from learning the appropriate behavioural skills – it's the behaviour of those who work with you, for you and even above you: bosses, too, need managing. Learning and applying new skills is an essential form of behaviour – one that, sadly, managers often abandon as they reach or near the summit. Mountaineers who did likewise would soon be dead climbers.

You can understand, though not approve, this reluctance to learn. These people are busy, self-important and too lofty to submit themselves to the learning disciplines imposed on others. That's one reason for the halting progress of Total Quality Management in the west. In my studies of TQM successes and failures, the former, alas, are in the minority. The successful few had one feature in common, though, which explained both their success and the failure of the others: all the effective programmes began at the top, not in a show of chief executive 'commitment', but in the use of TQM techniques to improve the measurable and measured quality of top management itself.

Bad or laggardly decision-making, for example, can do far more damage than a bad production layout. The true TQM company improves both processes. Everywhere in the organization everyone is involved in major and minor projects with the single aim of achieving and maintaining continuous improvement. The result is to raise skill levels throughout the organization, starting with the techniques of analysis, diagnosis, prognosis and cure on which TQM depends. The technical aspects of TQM, however, are less important than the philosophy it teaches: that everything which can be improved must be – and that means everything.

The most powerful aspect of TQM is that the development of the organization and that of the individual go hand-in-hand. The purpose of a Total Quality project is determined by the team, which may be a team of one person. The project automatically becomes a project of the organization as a whole. You don't have to adopt TQM to achieve this unity of commitment, though. It's the essence of the Learning Company or (the term I prefer) the Ideas Company. In these organizations, all the lessons and ideas are shared by the people who learn and think within their walls.

Ψ

In the business context, education and skills are not pursued for their own sake, but to achieve a purpose. That's a better word than 'vision' or even 'mission', because it enshrines the same positive pragmatism that Drucker teaches. His first element of effectiveness, as noted, is to do 'what needs to be done'. At a path-finding company I recently visited, much the same enquiry was phrased differently by the directors: 'What is this company for?' Either way, you end up with a purpose – a clear statement of what has to be done and why, and which can be communicated and understood.

The purpose determines what new skills need to be developed or acquired – or applied. Take Drucker's Seventh Element: running effective meetings. According to survey after survey, executives (even junior managers and professionals) spend more than half of every day meeting with others – for even a one-on-one talk is a meeting. How do you make your gatherings more effective? You start by considering the purpose – and you fit the meeting to the purpose.

Suppose that the purpose is to generate new ideas, the lifeblood of any company. Developing ideas and turning them into execution is the most important of all general skills. 'General' is the right word. Every sentient human being has ideas in profusion – waking life is impossible without them. It is also well known that many brains working in collaboration are more effective than a single brain, however brilliant. The late Francis Crick was a scientific genius; but the discovery of how DNA works – the secret of life – required contributions from many minds. The interplay between Crick and James Watson was only one of the intellectual combinations required.

All the above is true. Yet organizations customarily run on two entirely false antitheses: that the higher your position, the more important your ideas; and that new thinking – i.e. creativity – is a rare skill possessed by rare people who are born with this ineffable talent. So nobody else need bother to have new ideas, need they? Nobody considers it strange or wrong, either, if a meeting is dominated by the person with the highest rank (and loudest voice); or if most of the participants offer no ideas whatsoever.

If you don't use a skill, your ability will atrophy. So insist that, if ideas are the purpose of the meeting, all the participants come with (say) three ideas relevant to the subject. Take everybody in rotation, with no interruptions save for clarification, and apply only one other rule: no idea can be rubbished – everybody gets treated with respect. When all have spoken, the meeting discusses (not debates) the ideas to arrive at a consensus on how to proceed.

The skill of the chairman (or whatever the leader is called) lies in achieving the consensus, and never allowing inconclusive, rambling and (above all) acrimonious debate. Stick to the point of the meeting, and call time when the purpose has been accomplished. Model your behaviour on Drucker's favourite executive ('the most effective ... I have ever known'): Alfred Sloan, the true founder of General Motors, and the father of the modern 'Concept of the Corporation'.

That's the title of the 1934 book that spread the message of modern management and made Drucker's reputation. Sloan, who had given the author unprecedented access to GM, disliked the book and was stimulated to write his own My Years with General Motors as a kind of rebuttal. But Drucker's esteem for Sloan has plainly remained undimmed down the years. He recounted, 70 years on, how Sloan spent three days a week 'in formal meetings with a set membership' and another three days in informal meetings with individual executives or small groups.

Sloan started by stating the purpose (as recommended above) of the meeting. Like the oil magnate John D.Rockefeller I (who would listen to discussions lying on a couch with his eyes shut), Sloan 'rarely spoke except to clarify a confusing point' and never took notes. Both giants, however, listened intently and remembered what they heard – as proved by their pithy follow-up memos. One from Sloan, sent to all present, would summarize the discussion and its conclusions and record any work decided on, with deadline and name of the executive assigned to the work.

Sloan thus exemplifies what should really be another element of the effective executive. Although Drucker adds this injunction as something of an afterthought, he elevates it to a sovereign rule: LISTEN FIRST, SPEAK LAST.

An enormous number of words have been devoted to the verbal skills of active communication, including presentation, negotiation, report writing, etc. These are all important, teachable skills (in which most managers are unnecessarily deficient). But communication is a two-way process – and by definition you learn more from listening to others than from speaking yourself.

The aural skills are thus equal to the verbal ones. But nobody much writes books on listening, which gives the naturally good listener, like Sloan or Rockefeller, a wonderful advantage. The above anecdotes go to the heart of excellent behaviours. Since they worked so supremely well in the hands of the two titans, there's no reason why the same behaviours shouldn't succeed for you. Try this catechism:

- Do you agree that the Sloan-Rockefeller behaviours are a powerful and highly effective mode of conduct?

- Are they superior to your own *modus operandi*?

- If so, are you prepared to try this different approach – starting, say, by becoming a better listener?

- If so prepared, will you actually perform as ordained?

Developing skills is a matter of learning what to do, and then learning how to do it. But without action – doing it – the learning and know-how are useless. Action is the slippery area of management. The would-be mountaineers can all too easily lose their footing as plans run up against the realities of logistics and lapses. But there's no substitute for the exposure to actuality. That's why today's all-embracing trend, the big shift to project management, is so highly educational – in addition to being the most effective form of organization.

The simple idea is to select self-contained tasks that can be entrusted to a discrete, *ad hoc* group within the organization. The group is a self-organizing, self-managing body with its own empowered leadership and all the skills required by the work. The overall task can likewise be broken down into sub-tasks, each one of which can similarly be delegated. The role of the group leadership is to monitor progress in all aspects, to keep the entire project on track, and to satisfy the senior leaders, outside the group, that this is being done.

Reliance on project management, though unsung, has become widespread as the complexities of business have magnified and multiplied. This downstream revolution – which undermines the pillars of hierarchy and bureaucracy – goes a long way toward converting an organization into a Learning Company or an Ideas Company. Although you can certainly learn to think more creatively (as Edward de Bono has long taught), creativity also means turning ideas into effective action – which will certainly demand more ideas still.

Ψ

If you're an artist, or a writer, or some other single-handed professional, you're free to act as you will. But people working in organizations depend heavily on the creativity of their environment. This is generally so stultifying that Clayton M. Christensen, the supreme expert on why supreme companies fail, advises one and all to locate major innovatory projects right outside the organization.

That worked brilliantly at IBM in the ultra high-speed generation of the personal computer. But the pioneering zest of the spin-off PC team wasn't allowed to infect the parent organization, which duly sucked the PC operation back inside – and sucked away its vitality. The group had achieved near-monopoly in the marketplace. As that vanished, PC leadership passed first to Compaq, then to Dell – and IBM as a whole was forced into most painful restructuring (and selling out to China).

Yet the creative energies shown by the initial PC triumph were surely still alive within IBM; alive, but not well. The creative skills that are most notably found in young people need constant nourishment – above all, as noted, that which comes with use. The problem is to remove the obstructive practices that get in the way of the creative potential, the drive to learn, think and execute – and you dare not leave this removal to the men and women at the top. Their top-down management is the greatest villain of the piece, inimical to the free and full expression and implementation of ideas.

The consultancy Arthur D. Little once generated a superb book on innovation called *Breakthrough!* It could well have been called *Against the Organization*: every western innovator studied had been forced to fight through determined and mindless opposition. The examples included such world-beaters as the microwave oven and the Post-it pad, whose father, Art Fry, had to work all through one night to prove that the engineers were wrong, and that the product actually could be manufactured.

The positive cases, where the innovators and the company were both on the same side throughout, were Japanese: like the Sony Walkman and the transformation of the microwave from Raytheon's clumsy monster, suitable only for railroad use, to the universal kitchen gadget. The Japanese reputation as mere imitators is a western myth. Anyway, who believes that imitation is always 'mere'? Properly executed, it can be a life-saver and a rich source of learning.

A Japanese manager would rightly be astounded by the notion that, if somebody is bettering you, you should not adopt their improvement. After all, that is the essence of education and skill development. You learn from your betters and, if possible, improve on what you have learnt. The Japanese would be equally amazed at the notion that ideas are the prerogative of the top echelons. Their bottom-up approach creates a culture in which ideas can flourish across the whole company. You see this in the flood of entries in the Toyota suggestion scheme (all are accepted unless they would have a negative effect).

You see it, too, in the anecdote of the secretary in an underperforming Japanese semi-conductor plant; the only person, though everybody waited for trains at the nearby station, to perceive that vibrations from the railroad track might explain the factory's unacceptably low yields (they did). You see it in the internal trade show at which Sony's people display their latest technological advances, not to customers, but to each other.

You don't see this democracy of ideas at the typical western company. I once asked middle managers at a large retail chain in Britain how many levels of approval were required for a new product range. I was much encouraged by the speed of the process and the short chain of approval: their boss and his boss. My enthusiasm was curbed, though, when the leader said there was something else I should know: 'then the chairman visits one of the stores, sees the shirts, demands to know "who put this rubbish here?", and orders their removal'.

Yet that same chairman, asked what he would request if granted one wish, had told me like a shot: 'for my young managers to be more creative'. The democracy of ideas is inhibited not only by hierarchical totalitarianism, but by prejudice lower down – for instance, the familiar killing of ideas as 'Not Invented Here'. The insistence that any ideas must be internally generated only makes sense if the NIH-ers can argue (a) that nobody outside is capable of generating relevant ideas and (b) that, even if the outsiders are capable, the internal ideas will always be superior.

Since those arguments are clearly untenable, the answer must lie in emotional blockage. The bad idea is 'I will lose prestige if I admit, by following other people's ideas, that they are better than mine'. This emotion works internally as well as externally, and explains many of the difficulties that subordinates encounter in trying to get ideas past their superiors. Outsiders have the same problem. External strategic consultants, for example, get a sinking feeling whenever their approach to the chief executive is referred downwards to the director of strategy. The latter will find it easier to say 'no' than to let the CEO undercut his precious authority of expertise.

The best advice, though, is to ignore NIH and all the other difficulties and to press ahead with your ideas as best you may, by every means at your disposal. It's an uphill and often unsuccessful battle (even more chancy than mountaineering), and may involve exercising skills of diplomacy and its opposite – bloody-mindedness. You may get stuck in a snow hole for months rather than days. But without the determined exercise of willpower, you are conspiring in your own frustration. Don't let your personal skill-set be negated by the failure of others. For those skills will get you to the top of the mountain.

SUMMIT 2

- Be **diligent** and pay close **attention to detail** at all times.

- **Move forward** decisively, keenly **aware of the risks**, but using your skills to minimize them.

- **Plan** for all contingencies, always **asking 'What if ...?'** this or that happens (or both).

- **Experience things** for yourself – if you truly want to understand what's going on.

- Always **have clear purposes**: ask 'what needs to be done?' – then, above all, do it!

- Have the confidence to **find out how good you really are** by putting your abilities to the test.

- Become a fanatical **self-improver** in your personal behaviour and development.

- **Improve everything** in the organization that can be improved – and that will mean everything.

- Make this a Golden Rule: **listen first, speak last.**

- Don't let your personal skill-set be negated by the **failings of others**.

Moving with the Flow

It was on the return journey from Denali that the idea of the Seven Summits first entered my mind. The conversation among my travelling companions had turned to various peaks in far-flung corners of the world they had climbed, or more to the point, they wanted to climb. Interspersed in the excited chat were names foreign and unfamiliar to me, some names that frankly I could barely wrap my tongue around: Aconcagua, Carstensz Pyramid, Elbrus and Vinson – the highest peaks, it turned out, in the respective continents of South America, Australasia, Europe and Antarctica.

My interest sharpened. Hadn't I climbed the highest peak in Africa, and now North America? The following year we were booked to climb the highest mountain in the world, which, for the sake of this conversation, also happened to be the highest in Asia. What if I were to continue and climb the full complement of seven – the highest peak on each of the seven continents? Wouldn't that be the most perfect excuse to travel the world?

So it was that the idea of climbing the Seven Summits was hatched. Two down. One booked for the following year and four remaining to stack up as wild adventures for some time in the future. It was a dream, beyond my existing dream to climb Everest. But first I had to realize that first ambition. Without one I couldn't have the other.

Ψ

We returned from Denali in May 1992 and were set to leave for Everest the following March. We had ten months to prepare, and as time ticked by a concern that I had kept buried deep in my subconscious bubbled to the forefront of my mind: I couldn't climb Everest while in the office. Would my employers grant me three months leave?

I sensed the answer might be 'no', even before I asked the question. Times were tough, I was told. I had the choice of keeping my job or climbing Everest.

For many, it might have been the physical risks inherent in climbing a mountain that would be the greatest challenge. But for me it was the risk of unemployment the other side of Everest that was my greatest fear.

Nonetheless, my mind was made up in an instant – I *must* go to Everest. In my heart I didn't see that I had any choice. Everest had become an all-consuming passion in my life; I had walked too far along the path towards it to step aside now. Quite simply, I didn't have it in me to watch the opportunity slip by.

Yet, how was I going to pay the mortgage? Would I find a job on my return?

I remember the moment my boss broke the news to me. I slipped on my coat and walked along the alleyway alongside our office building, and sat for a while in the local café. I'll sell my car, I thought. Let my flat. I'll eat lentils if it comes to it. *Somehow I will make it work.*

Of course, it is easy to say in hindsight, but in many ways signing a letter of resignation, as I did, was the best decision I have ever made in my life. The lesson is, that to follow one's chosen path takes commitment – a good deal of it. Often it will require a sacrifice – to give up a job, or to invest a large sum of money, or to move home, perhaps. But the rewards in terms of fulfilment are potentially huge.

That isn't to say that the moment of commitment – and sacrifice – isn't accompanied by a good dollop of fear. I was very, very frightened when I gave up my job. But experience tells me that we work through periods of fear, acclimatize to uncertainty and develop new confidence. I still feel butterflies in my stomach when I take a new challenge on board, but now I welcome that feeling because I know it is a preliminary to a period of change and growth. As Susan Jeffers so brilliantly entitled her book, *Feel the Fear and Do It Anyway.*

A welcome bonus is that the moment of commitment can also be accompanied by the most liberating feeling in the world. It is the moment when a true awareness of what you want to do – the path in life you want to follow – comes together with the realization that you have the power within you to actually do something about it. All of a sudden you are moving with the flow of the river instead of frantically paddling against it, because all your actions are driven by your wants. You might tumble over a waterfall or two, or be stuck for a while in some stagnant backwater, but as long as you are on the right path for you, gravity will be on your side.

One more thing: when you take a leap of faith and walk a path aligned to your desires, other people recognize your authenticity and want to help. No longer battling with yourself, you are no longer battling with the world – and everything flows with considerably less resistance.

Trusting to Teamwork 1

EVEREST, 8,848M (29,028FT)

Straddling the border of Nepal and Tibet, Everest's massive pyramid stands head and shoulders above its surrounding peaks in the Himalayas and is the highest mountain in the world. In Nepal it is called Sagamartha, 'Goddess of the Sky'; and in Tibet, Chomolungma, 'Goddess Mother of the Earth.' Its English name was given in honour of Sir George Everest, British surveyor general of India from 1830 to 1843.

Mystery still surrounds early Everest mountaineers George Mallory and Andrew 'Sandy' Irvine, who were last seen high on Everest's North East Ridge 'still going strong for the summit' on 8 June 1924, 'before being enveloped in cloud.' But the first indisputable ascent was by Sir Edmund Hillary and Sherpa Tenzing Norgay on 29 May 1953. Medical professionals argued that Everest's summit was beyond the reach of human capabilities. They were proved wrong, but still its extreme altitude stretches even the most competent climbers to their limits.

I was under no illusion; Everest was to be by far the greatest mountaineering challenge I had faced to date. If ever there was a time that I needed to be rock sure of my path, Everest was it. Yet the profound lesson I learned from this highest mountain in the world wasn't one of blind determination fuelled by the desire of an individual (although that naturally played a part), but one of the collective power of a team of people working together.

So sure am I now of the strength of people coming together that it seems to me remote that I could have thought any other way. But the fact is that prior to my experience on Everest the very word 'team' made me feel a little ill at ease. I lived on my own in those days, and took a certain pride in my independence. I was largely self-contained, and self-sufficient. I could manage my own affairs (so I thought) and choose to see friends and family when it suited me. 'Teamwork' smacked a little too much of 'chumminess'; also of dependency on others, and vulnerability.

But how long could I be in denial? We all need to interact with others to maintain our health and sanity. And as for Everest? Without other people my dream to climb it would have remained just that: a dream. I would never have left my flat in London.

What I appreciate now (slow to face the obvious) is that nothing of any scale or significance is achieved on our own. We live in family groups and communities. We work in companies comprising tens, hundreds, even thousands of people; and although one individual might be a spokesperson or representative of a group's collective work, that person will be keenly aware that his or her success is in no small part due to the efforts and dynamics of the team.

In the simplest of terms, a team allows a number of individuals each to contribute different skills to a pot; although the lesson that I drew from Everest was a different and far more exciting one. The lesson from Everest was about the support and inspiration that each person in a team draws from the others – and also gives to the others – and how, with a common aim and purpose, barriers that most commonly separate individuals can be knocked down, unleashing a wave of energy that makes the seemingly impossible possible.

Teamwork, I learned, isn't about dependency as once I'd feared. It's about interdependency, drawing strength and relying upon one another while also supporting and inspiring one another. It's about give and take. Sometimes one individual feels the stronger; at other times, another. And together – provided everyone pulls in the same direction – a good deal more is achieved than if the same individuals act in isolation.

Ψ

My first taste of the effectiveness of teamwork came right at the start of the climb, on our first ascent through the infamous Khumbu Icefall. I had never seen the icefall before, except in books, and in my imagination. As a reporter I had approached Everest from the north, through Tibet, and so avoided it. As a climber I was approaching it from the south, through Nepal. Here the Khumbu Icefall stands as a terrifying and imposing obstacle above the Base Camp: we had no choice but to climb through the icefall if we were to enter a high hanging valley called the Western Cwm, and from there to climb to the South Col and in turn, the summit.

On reflection, I think it's possible that I could have completed the trek through the foothills of the Himalayas to the Base Camp without the support of my friends; but through the Khumbu Icefall? Inconceivable. The icefall is a twisting, tumbled labyrinth of ice – over 700 vertical metres of vast ice blocks stacked one on top of another, formed where the Khumbu Glacier, lying flat and sedate on the floor of the Western Cwm, topples over the lip of Cwm and cascades to the valley floor below. It is like a waterfall – one of Niagara proportions – except that it comprises ice.

Stand in its shadow for an hour or even two and you might mistakenly be led to believe that one block of ice is frozen securely to another; that en masse it is immovable, cemented soundly to the underlying rock. But hang around for half a day or so, or lie restless at its base through the night, and you will know differently. You will hear it creak and groan. You will hear ear-splitting cracks and disturbing rumbles as sections of it collapse and avalanche. The force of gravity is at play on it night and day; it takes no rest – and slowly the icefall grinds its way to the valley floor.

I had heard the stories of its victims – people lost in its gaping crevasses, or crushed in a toppling jungle of ice. These people weren't ill-prepared; just unlucky. To climb through the icefall is to play a game of Russian roulette. It was the one obstacle above all others that I feared might stop me in my tracks, before I had even set foot on the mountain. And my point is that I know it would have done; no doubt about it. Except that I was in the company of people I trusted.

The morning of our first climb through the icefall I stood nervously in the mess tent with the others, gulping tepid lemon juice, fiddling with my harness straps and generally distracting myself from the task that lay ahead. It was early, about 4 a.m., and I'd had a bad night, unable to rid my mind of worry. It was now adrenalin that fuelled my actions. My heart beat heavily in my chest. I breathed deeply in an attempt to calm my uneasy movements. Couldn't people see that I was scared? Weren't they scared? Looking about me it seemed that climbing this monstrous icefall was a challenge my companions undertook every day. There was a collective air of calm. Could it be simply that they disguised their anxieties well? I will probably never know the answer to that question, but one thing that I understood implicitly at the time was that I must not surrender to my fear, or I'd lose the plot. Fear, like courage, spreads like wildfire through a crowd.

Our time came. We put down our empty mugs, turned our headlamps to full beam and filed out of the tent one after the other, and walked in single file towards the icefall. Even this I don't suppose I would have managed on my own. Before long I was strapping crampons to my boots. Then I was climbing a gradient towards the icefall, then *in* the icefall, among great boulders of ice – weaving under them, around them, up faces of them, and stepping gingerly along rickety aluminium ladders cast over dark, gaping chasms that lay between them. My sensory system was still on high alert, but I was making progress, biting off one great chunk of the icefall after another – until, several hours on, the sun rising in the sky, I climbed a string of ladders cast up and over the lip of the icefall into the Western Cwm. I had done it. My companions hadn't pushed me, or dragged me, or carried me; but what they had done was to cradle me psychologically from the start to the end. This is just one example of the strength derived from working with a team; one example of why I can say categorically that I could never have climbed Everest alone.

Once through the icefall, the journey to the summit of Everest takes a climber along the length of the Western Cwm – a valley virtually flat but for a gentle incline at the end – then up the steep, icy Lhotse Face to the South Col, and from there, up the final summit pyramid to the top. From Base Camp to summit, it is a distance of some six and a half miles; and much more relevant, a vertical interval of 3,500m. We had four camps above the Base Camp: Camp 1 at the top of the Khumbu Icefall; Camp 2 on a strip of lateral moraine at the head of the Western Cwm; Camp 3 pitched precariously on a dug-out ledge some half way up the Lhotse Face; and Camp 4, our highest camp, on the South Col.

There were a number of obstacles on this journey, toing and froing between the various camps that would have been impossible for me to overcome without both the psychological and practical support of the other climbers on the team. Indeed, I can say categorically that there wasn't a single person in the team who wasn't instrumental in some way or another to the success of those of us who reached the summit. But in this text I am going to focus only on one further section of the climb: that is the crux of the climb, from our high camp on the South Col to the summit and, of course, back down again. And by nature of the fact that on this summit pyramid of Everest there were fewer players than at the base, I will be focusing on relationships with only a handful of key players, most notably the leader, John Barry, and three very special Sherpas: Ang Passang, Kami Tchering and Tcheri Zhambu.

Ψ

First, the summit pyramid: the crux of the climb. It is commonly said that Everest isn't a very difficult climb; it is just a bit too high. No truer words could be spoken.

The height of Everest is 8,848m (29,028ft). In a measurement that might be easier to visualize, that is almost nine kilometres or five and half miles high. Jet planes cruise at about the level of its summit. The problem with this isn't simply a matter of scale; it isn't that a climber need take more steps to reach its summit than on a lesser peak. The problem is one of the environment close to and on the summit, which is dangerously inhospitable due to two geophysical laws. The first is that with increasing height the levels of oxygen are reduced; and the second, that with increasing height the ambient air temperature falls. Neither of which are terribly helpful to human beings. On the summit, the level of oxygen is one third of that at sea level – nowhere near enough to sustain life. And if people choose to visit such lofty heights – which of course they must if they are to climb Everest – then they do so in the knowledge that their bodies, weakened by the lack of oxygen, will be dangerously vulnerable to the cold.

The fact is that most climbers will suffer the detrimental effects of altitude long before they climb anywhere near the pyramidal summit. Nausea, headaches, difficulty in sleeping, suppressed appetite and weight loss are the norm. And in addition there are risks of pulmonary and cerebral oedema, frostbite and hypothermia. But above the South Col – generally, above 8,000m or so – risks of falling victim to the altitude reach critical levels.

As a rule of thumb, climbers intent on scaling Everest by way of the South Col and South East Ridge set out from the high camp on the col in the middle of the night and aim to complete the round trip – to the summit and back to the South Col – by nightfall the following day. If, for whatever reason, they fail to keep to this schedule and are forced to overnight without supplementary oxygen and any means of shelter high on the mountain, then their chances of survival are small. People have survived such an ordeal, but rarely; they are the exception to prove the rule.

You might ask why on earth climbers wouldn't carry some spare oxygen in case of such an eventuality, or indeed a tent, or a sleeping bag. The reason is quite simply that to carry such an extra burden would so slow them down that they couldn't hope to meet their objective and reach the summit.

Above the South Col you are truly out on a limb. Helicopters can't fly that high, for anyone wondering.

In the duration of our stay on the mountain, five people lost their lives. None died through accidents in the Khumbu Icefall, or on the Lhotse Face, but all in that area inimical to man above the South Col. One I shall never be able to forget. It was early in the season – in April, still – and a Nepalese woman successfully made it to the summit. Her name was Pasang Lhamu Sherpa and she was the first woman of her country to climb Everest. Those of us still at the Base Camp received news of her ascent through her support team, but the reaction wasn't one of celebration – rather, anxious concern. Her ascent had apparently been slow and she was forced to overnight close to the summit. A Sherpa stayed with her in support. The next morning brought no news and we feared the worst. The following day there was still no news and we knew the worst. Both Pasang Lhamu and the Sherpa had died. They hadn't had an accident or taken a fall; they were simply too high for too long. It is the reason that the higher reaches of Everest above the South Col are known dramatically, yet poignantly, as the Death Zone.

To climb through the Death Zone – up and back down the top 950m – is, galling though it may seem when the possible consequences are considered, what it is all about. This is the challenge; and a small group of us were there – high up on the South Col – ready to meet that challenge on 9 May.

The first half of May is the most favourable period of the year for climbing Everest, and as a consequence we were far from being alone. A number of expeditions from every imaginable corner of the world – expeditions that had pitched their tents next to ours at the Base Camp and at Camps 1, 2 and 3 – were now with us at the highest camp, eager to make a bid for the summit. It was a scene deceptive of its seriousness: the sky was a rich, deep blue; a colony of state-of-the-art, brilliantly coloured tents – red, yellow, silver – were pitched on the arid rocks brightening an otherwise desolate col; and climbers, donned in equally garish gear, stood nonchalantly chatting to one another, or else clasping radios, as if conducting business on mobile phones.

Within this crowd we formed a small group of six. There was John, the leader; the two doctors on the expedition, Sandy Scott and Andy Peacock; two Sherpas, Ang Passang and Kami Tchering, and me. And there was also a seventh, a climber who was a part of our expedition but nonetheless climbing independently. His name was Harry Taylor. The previous day he had been climbing with three others in the team who, like him, had been keen to attempt an ascent without supplementary oxygen, but who, on the climb to the South Col, had got caught in bad weather and retreated. Harry, a gifted climber at high altitudes, had forged ahead of them and managed to safely ensconce himself in his tent on the South Col before the weather deteriorated. So he was there, too, already an old hand on the col, smiling as he greeted us on our arrival.

Ψ

It was my assumption, because it is the normal strategy of things, that having arrived on the South Col early in the afternoon we might rest awhile and set out for the summit in the evening of that same day, at about 11.00 p.m. At this altitude there is no advantage in resting for any longer because the detrimental effect on one's body of the rarefied air is greater than any benefit that might be derived from sleep.

The weather forecast pointed at a quick ascent as well. It was for winds of 22 knots and temperatures of -32° C – not perfect, but markedly better than for the following two days when the winds were forecast to be progressively stronger.

But how wrong could I have been?

'You can go, but we're staying,' said Sandy.

Andy, our respiratory specialist, wasn't faring well. His movements were slow and his logic seemingly amiss. He was reluctant to tuck himself into his sleeping bag, for example, despite the cold, and remarkably slow to respond to requests to zip up the tent. It's probable that he suffered a mild oedema.

Still, John and I could go with the Sherpas.

'You're exhausted,' said John. 'Andy's sick and it's windy,' which indeed it was; the wind picked up as darkness fell. 'And that,' he bellowed, 'is that!'

I was incensed with him. He wouldn't even open the subject to discussion, and I had no choice but to lie there in the tent, witnessing an opportunity slip away.

At about 11.00 p.m. Harry, who had clearly decided to give it a go, was to be heard shuffling outside the tent. He called out to John through the canvas: 'John, your Sherpas want to go.' John grunted and rolled over to sleep. An hour or so later and there was further disturbance outside; this time, climbers from another expedition preparing themselves for an ascent. I could hear them chatting, the inimitable sound of tent zips opening and closing as they stepped outside into the dark, and the scraping of metal crampons on rock. I sat bolt upright: 'John, we must go!'

But it was to no avail. The following morning the two doctors, Andy and Sandy, decided to call it a day and made their way back down the Lhotse Face to the Western Cwm. John, Ang Passang, Kami Tchering and I decided to stay. Maybe, we thought – maybe if we were lucky – we would have a chance to give it a go ourselves that night.

It was a long day waiting for our turn on the South Col, and, as it turned out, a crucifying one. A good number of the climbers who had set out from the South Col the previous night had succeeded in making it to the summit. The weather had turned good, after all.

During the course of the afternoon I watched one figure after another descend from the higher reaches of Everest and walk tired but contentedly, with an air of pride, into camp. I watched and watched. Dusk fell and still I watched, until slowly the trickle of climbers stopped.

I tried desperately to control my feelings of disappointment. After all, this emotion wasn't going to get me to the top. I tried to turn it around, to think positively about the opportunity that lay ahead of us. But before long all thoughts of disappointment, or indeed hope, were shunted out of my brain to be replaced with a concern far more serious. Where was Harry?

I succeeded in harbouring my anxiety for a while until, sitting and waiting in the tent with John, I could bear it no longer and burst out: 'Harry must have had an accident.' In the very delivery of the words it seemed that it must be a reality.

I looked out of the tent, up at the pyramidal summit again and again, until once, peering into the darkness, I caught sight of a light – a head torch, for sure – not so very far from the South Col. I watched intently. It didn't move. 'Flash the torch,' suggested John; and I did so, six times. Harry had been in the SAS and would certainly know this international distress signal, but there was no response from whoever was the owner of the head torch.

Suddenly, in the nervous tension that filled our tent, our alarm clock screamed. It was 10.00 p.m. Harry had been on the hill for 23 hours, far longer than could be expected. Adrenalin surged through my body. It's hard to explain how helpless one feels on a big mountain, in the dark, at such altitudes. Where would we begin to look? I flashed up the stove and reached for a boot: 'We've got to do something.' Then, one boot securely zipped to my foot, I looked outside to see the light of two head torches pan over a nearby tent. I heard voices, and then saw the two lights move in the direction of the lone light, positioned not so very far from the South Col. 'We'll wait and see what happens, then go,' said John. There was nothing else to do. John was up and out of the tent as the lights moved back towards the camp. As they drew closer, three shapes emerged in the shadows. And there, before our eyes, were two figures, upright and able, dragging a third figure, slumped on the ground. 'British people, British people,' I heard someone cry, 'we have your friend, he is dying.'

It would be convenient to say that Harry was the reason that John and I never made a bid for the summit that night; but it wouldn't be the whole truth. We wanted, of course, to look after Harry, but the wind picked up and only got worse as the long night drew on.

Ψ

Harry had made it to the top. His problem was that he had contracted snow blindness. The intense ultra-violet light, unfiltered at such altitudes, scorched his eyes and stole his sight. He fell, lost a crampon, and fell again – 30m or so – to the place not so very far from the South Col where the two climbers – Spanish, both – found him floundering in the snow and dragged him back to safety.

The night that followed was one of the most horrendous of my life, but also one of the most extraordinary. I was never quite able to accustom myself to the violence of storms, and the wind howled in eerie screams that night. Great gusts of wind blew full force at our tent, whipping the canvas in deafening cracks and threatening to buckle the poles. My fingers were continuously on the verge of freezing. Yet there was a certainty of focus in ensuring that Harry had enough to eat, and more important, to drink, that awakened something deeply primal in me. It was a need to be needed – an emotion both deeply rewarding and enriching.

The slightly puzzling thing about that night is that, despite Harry's burning eyes, and despite his bruises and obvious discomfort, I still looked at him stretched out in his sorry state and thought: 'you lucky, lucky man'. The fact is that I was deeply envious of him, for he had climbed his Everest and I hadn't so much as placed a foot above the South Col.

On balance, it's important to have such burning ambition if the aim is to achieve something that is to stretch you beyond your known limits. But I realize now that ambition must be tempered; it must be examined with an objective eye. Standing back from Everest, I know that I took risks within sight of the summit that I never would have taken given distance and a quiet time to reason. The summit has a magnetic draw which only increases in power as you climb closer to it; and in one sense it could be argued that this is a good thing, because you need an extra burst of drive to push through the toughest final steps. But a climber needs to be wary and focus not just on the summit but also on what lies beyond, or else the result might be a successful ascent but a failure to descend. A pyrrhic victory, you could say.

The same is true for the mountains we climb in our business and personal lives: we want success, but not at the expense of our family, health, loyalty and trust of our colleagues and friends.

As it happened, the following morning on the South Col, as the day awakened and with relief we watched the canvas of our tent metamorphose from dark mustard to a bright yellow, we felt no such temptation to strike blindly for the summit. The winds were ferocious and we had no choice but to head down.

The Sherpas Ang Passang and Kami Tchering stood outside our tent. 'You go with them', John insisted. He would stay. Harry still wasn't able to see and needed looking after.

So, the three of us, holding hands – tiny figures in a high and desolate wilderness – leant full body weight into the wind and fought our way across the South Col; until, with relief, we clambered over the crest of the Geneva Spur and onto the heavily snow laden slopes of the Lhotse Face and out of the prevailing wind.

Ψ

I fell into the cook tent at Camp 2, utterly spent. The Sherpas had raced ahead of me and were sitting on rocks that passed as seats, eating a meal. I had thought they, like me, would rest for a while at Camp 2 – await John and Harry's safe arrival – but now, looking at the urgency in their movement, I realized to my dismay that their intent was to continue apace down through the Khumbu Icefall to Base Camp, and home. It was written in their eyes: they'd had enough of the mountains for a year; they wanted to see their wives and their children, drink cold beer and breathe thick, moisture-laden air.

And where would that leave us? I couldn't deny that we'd had a setback; that the expectations of many would be that we should call it a day. But we must climb back up to the South Col and give it another go, mustn't we? And how were we going to do that without the support of the Sherpas?

In a moment of rare clarity I realized that I had to act immediately. Once the Sherpas finished their meal they would be up and off; and if I stayed at Camp 2 I might never see them again. So I lifted my exhausted body and moved to sit beside them. 'Please don't go home', I said, 'We need you here. Please, please come back up the mountain when you're rested'.

The Sherpas nodded but without conviction; the expression in their eyes didn't change. Then, having finished their meal, they left. I waved them off believing I would never see them again.

The days that followed were a heady mix of the most extreme emotions. After a further night on the South Col John successfully managed to aid Harry down the Lhotse Face and my overriding feeling – like that of all of us on the team – was one of relief. Harry's eyes were on the mend; his only injury was a touch of frostbite on one of his toes, and within a day or two he was fit and well enough to climb back down the icefall to the Base Camp.

There was a sense of pride, too, that Harry had made it to the top. His personal success was a success for the team as well, and we might have been justified in congratulating ourselves and heading for home. Indeed, all around us, that is exactly what people were doing. Expeditions from America, New Zealand and Spain were loading rucksacks and heading down. The whole flow of traffic was downhill; and yet, desperately, I wanted to climb back up.

Rarely have I felt my heart and my head in such a battle. I still badly wanted to climb to the summit; my desire hadn't diminished. But the rational part of my being argued that I didn't stand a chance. Everything seemed to be loaded against me. I was tired. We had been at altitudes of 6,700m (22,000ft) for a period approaching three weeks and as a result I was stick thin (two stones, I lost, my limbs rattling in what had been skin-tight clothes), as well as emotionally drained.

We were running out of time physically, mentally – and seasonally. It was already mid-May and by the end of the month we could expect the onset of the monsoon with its heavy snowfall and associated risk of avalanche. And to cap it all, the immediate weather forecast – transmitted by satellite from Bracknell to Base Camp – was for high winds: 45 pushing 50 knots. If Bracknell's forecast was right, there was no way we could inch our way along the precipitous, shark-fin ridge that leads to the summit.

It was bleak. I felt convinced that if we were to climb the Lhotse Face once more, we would be climbing into failure. We might make it to the South Col, but the winds would drive us back down again. Our chance of success, I put at about one in a hundred.

I hardly dared seek the opinion of others for I sensed already a degree of reticence; that to give it another go didn't make any sense; that we should call it a day and be satisfied.

There was only one person on the team who was actually prepared and able to give it another go, and that was the leader of the team, John. He had been resting up in his tent for a couple of days, recuperating from his ordeal on the South Col. I don't believe I fully appreciated it at the time, but on reflection I realize that it was remarkable that he even contemplated another attempt. Three nights he had spent on the South Col, the last in a storm of such ferocity that it threatened to rip the anchors from the tent. John stockpiled essential provisions and stuffed them in a sack – water, food, gloves, hats – so that should he and Harry find themselves stranded in the Death Zone without a tent, they could at least fight for survival behind a rock. He rationed his oxygen, not knowing when, or if, the storm would subside in time to assist Harry down. Several times he'd had, as he put it, 'long conversations with his maker'.

Yet, on the afternoon of 15 May, 1993, he packed his rucksack and donned his boots, ready for another go. The two of us set out from Camp 2 and headed across the glacier, our plan being to climb to Camp 3, stay overnight, and the following day climb to the South Col, from there to summit on 17 May. But we didn't even reach the foot of the Lhotse Face. In stepping out – in placing one foot in front of the other – John was forced to acknowledge something that I suspect he already knew: that in saving Harry's life he had jeopardized his chance of climbing Everest. Together we turned about and returned to camp.

Ψ

This might well have been the closure of my attempt on Everest. It is inconceivable that I might have climbed it on my own; even if physically able, psychologically I wouldn't have mustered the courage. It would have been the end of the road, then – but for one very important event. Sherpas Ang Passang and Kami Tchering decided, for reasons that shall always remain their own, that they would give up the idea of returning to their families for a little while longer and climb back up to Camp 2, ready and awaiting should we decide to give it another go. And for that I will thank them until the end of my days; their actions gave me hope once more.

There was another Sherpa, too, not to be left out. His name was Tcheri Zhambu. He was the youngest of the group – only twenty – and less experienced as a consequence, but able and keen. And we decided that, should we make another attempt, it would be the four of us who set out from Camp 2.

We had left it too late to go that same day. We would have to leave early the following morning and yet still aim to summit on 17 May because of the deteriorating weather. (The forecast for 17 May was for winds of 45 knots – not good, but better than the progressively stronger winds forecast for 18 and 19 May.) This meant that a journey to the South Col that had previously taken us a couple of days would have to be covered in a single day, direct from Camp 2.

The decision – whether or not we should go – wasn't any easier to make with the passing of time. I still feared that we would be climbing into failure, that our chance of success was no more than one in a hundred.

When I look back on this time it sometimes feels to me that the decision might very easily have swung either way; that we could as readily have decided not to go, as to go – as if on a toss of a coin. But in fact there was some strong reasoning behind the decision made. On one side of the coin I felt that our chances of success were infinitesimally small; but the flip side was far grimmer: to give up, to go home and not to know whether we might have made it for one last concerted effort. I didn't want to lie in bed at home in London and ask, ' What if … what if we had climbed back up to the South Col and Bracknell was wrong, it wasn't so windy after all?'

There are always some things that are outside our control in life. On a mountain it is very clearly the weather. In business it might be a downturn in the economic climate, interest rates, competition, war. But there are also a whole lot of things within our control, and on Everest I wanted to ensure that I had done absolutely everything possible within my power to make it to the top. If the weather stopped me, so be it; I would accept it. But if I failed because of my own lassitude? That I would have to live with for the rest of my life.

Ang Passang, Kami Tchering, Tcheri Zhambu and I were up at 3.30 a.m., as were John and Sandy and Nawang, the Sherpa cook. I felt tremendously indebted to everybody on the team who had waited on our decision so patiently, who had administered the repositioning of food and oxygen, relayed us forecasts, and now dragged themselves from the warmth of their sleeping bags into the cold darkness of the early hours to support us and to see us off.

I will admit that I still felt a degree of despondency. Was there really any point? Slowly I ploughed my way through a plate of rice that Nawang had prepared for me, taking smaller and smaller mouthfuls, delaying the inevitable. Before long Tcheri Zhambu was ready and waiting for me. John and Sandy were waiting for me, too, and I knew, if I were to maintain a modicum of pride, I could delay no longer.

'It'll be a monumental test of will', John said of the climb that lay ahead of us. And he was right – though not completely.

As it turned out it wasn't the climb itself that was difficult. Almost from the moment I stepped onto the snow-laden glacier in the Western Cwm, I found a rhythm, a lightness of foot and of heart. My fears and my despondency all but dissipated, to be replaced with a deep contentment that we were doing everything that it was possible to do. And with this load off my mind I was free to enjoy the view, and climb just for the pleasure of climbing.

What had been difficult were the agonizing days it took to make the decision and the summoning of the energy to pack my rucksack, don my harness, boots and crampons, and take that first step onto the hill once more.

Action kills fear. Deliberation is sometimes difficult to avoid. It is often an unavoidable part of the decision-making process – important in order to consider all the various factors and options. But there can be a confidence in knowing that when the time comes to act, nothing will be as bad as feared.

We made good progress up the Lhotse Face – familiar ground this time – and by early afternoon we were settled on the South Col. There were no crowds to suggest an air of joviality this time; and our tents, once domed in shape, were decidedly deflated and battered.

'The forecast for 11.00 p.m. tonight is for winds picking up 35 to 40 knots and then tomorrow (our summit day) going up to 45 knots', said our friend Peter Earl over the radio. Nothing new there. 'It's not good', he said. 'And tomorrow they're talking about thundery showers, so if you go up you've really got to get down fast before the really nasty weather comes in. Over.'

'Thanks Peter. Over.'

Ψ

There was little we could do, other than to rest the best we could, and wait. My memory of that time is of a brief interlude of relaxation, helped by the fact that I was in such wonderful company. The Sherpas are characteristically gentle, fun-loving, generous people, and Tcheri Zhambu – my tent companion – was no exception. Under normal circumstances I might make an effort to help with the domestic chores around the tent; but that afternoon it was Tcheri Zhambu who manned the radio, sorted the oxygen, sparked the stove and collected and melted snow, and prepared us a bite to eat. I offered to help but he wouldn't allow me to, and I didn't argue.

At about 7.00 p.m. we put our heads down for a few hours. I didn't sleep, just rested, ears open to the goings-on around.

'Tcheri Zhambu', I whispered.

He stirred.

'Tcheri Zhambu, there's no wind.'

I could hardly believe our luck. The canvas of our tent was absolutely still, silent. There wasn't a whisper of wind. 'Bracknell', I said, 'is wrong.'

Tcheri Zhambu sat bolt upright and immediately lit the stove and started to prepare drinks. It's slow business, collecting and melting snow, and about an hour passed before I sensed that my optimism for the summit might be misplaced. Tcheri Zhambu, and Ang Passang and Kami Tchering in the other tent, were talking to one another in Nepali.

'What's going on?' I asked Tcheri Zhambu.

'Weather's not good.'

'But there's no wind', I retorted. Looking out of the tent, up to the summit pyramid of Everest, the view was perfectly clear; the sky crowded with stars.

'Ang Passang says black cloud in valley. Too dangerous', said Tcheri Zhambu.

I will admit that on hearing this news a large part of me thought: what a perfect excuse, I can crawl back into my sleeping bag, put my head down and forget the whole idea.

The mind can oscillate wildly from one extreme to the other when the pressure's on, when the body's fatigued and the outcome of one's efforts looks uncertain. It is like a duel between the positive and negative parts of one's being, battling it out. On a couple of occasions when I have felt under extreme stress – stepping out onto a sheer, exposed ice-wall; or jumping out of a plane with a parachute – I have heard two distinct, crystal-clear voices arguing in my head. 'You're going to die!' 'No everything will be just fine.' The secret is to take a deep breath and step back from the situation, refocus on the summit (or the flight!) in one's mind's eye, grasp the positive argument and repeat it over and over, and banish the negativity aside.

'Ang Passang, pass the radio please.'

John and Sandy had made a point of sleeping in the cook tent that night, by the radio, should I need to call them for reassurance or advice.

I explained: 'John, Ang Passang says it's dangerous. He says the cloud is too black, we may not find our way, and there's lightning. Do you have a view on that?'

'I don't know, Becks.' This was desperate. 'The weather's going to get worse, not necessarily in the next two hours, but it's going to build up. Whether it will hold off long enough I wouldn't like to say.'

We deliberated for a period of an hour or so, until the radio batteries nearly ran flat. Should we climb, or not? The problem, of course, was that nobody could say with any authority what the weather was going to do. If the storm moved up from the valley onto the South East Ridge, then we would have a dangerous situation on our hands. But it might as easily drift off in the opposite direction.

'Talk it over very gently with Ang Passang and let him make the final decision,' said John. 'It's his life, too.'

John displayed remarkable courage that night. He, better than anybody, understood the dangers that lay above the South Col – and bad weather would only compound them. My guess is that he knew, too, that we would take heed of his advice; and that if he suggested that we should go and the worst happened and we shouldn't return, then he, as leader, would be held responsible. He would be the one at whom difficult questions would be fired by the climbing fraternity, by the media (for newspapers were onto the story by this stage), and by my family. 'What am I going to tell your mum?' was a plea he cried a couple of times during the course of our conversation.

It would have been very easy for John simply to say, 'Call it a day, Becks; it's not worth the risk.' But he didn't, because he understood how important it was for me to give it the best shot I could.

As we waited – still unsure of what to do – the weather remained calm on the col, and stars still crowded the sky above our heads. Then, in the darkness, I spotted three head torches beaming in a line, slowly moving across the South Col in the direction of the slopes leading towards the summit. The sight of the lights triggered my memory: they must be those of the three tiny figures I had spotted far below us, climbing the Lhotse Face earlier in the day.

I can't recall the exact moment we decided that we would give it a go as well; but one thing I knew for certain: if these three people thought there might be even the slimmest chance of making it to the summit, I couldn't retire back to bed.

Ψ

12.30 a.m. and we were ready to go: water bottles, chocolate, gloves, glasses, radio, camera, crampons on, ice-axe in hand, oxygen on back, mask on face. 'Get on those ropes', said John. 'Get onto the South Summit. Reassess the situation there. And good luck. I think you're going to be OK. Over.'

Just as he was leaving I heard him switch his attention to Base Camp. 'The beauty of fixed ropes', he said, 'is that you can't get lost. If the worse comes to the worst they can just turn round and rattle down the ropes back to the tent.'

The Sherpas and I walked into the darkness, one behind the other. The South Col itself is virtually flat, leading to gentle slopes that gradually steepen into a gully that leads straight up the face and then to the right, onto the South East Ridge. We had hardly climbed 200 metres when Tcheri Zhambu, the youngest of the Sherpas, declared that he had to turn back. He had contracted a hacking cough – a common ailment in the dry, abrasive air – and couldn't go on.

So in the end it was just the three of us – Ang Passang, Kami Tchering and me – who continued on our way. The going was steep, much steeper than I had imagined. Our crampons stabbed blue ice, sparked on bare rock, or else sank deep into freshly fallen snow. I wondered how John would have felt if he knew what we were about to discover: that there were no fixed ropes, or if so, they were buried deep beneath the snow.

We continued on. A thin cloud now hung in the sky; the stars no longer visible. Nonetheless, I could see high above us, in the shadows, the snowy gully that led to the South East Ridge, and, closer now, three head torches burning. We were doing all right, I thought. Making progress. Except that the Sherpas, I was to learn shortly, felt otherwise. It was about 4.00 a.m., still dark, and the two of them sat down on a precariously angled shelf of snow, and refused to budge.

'What's the matter, guys?'

Once again they were chatting in Nepali, this time on the radio. They passed it to me.

'Becks?'

It was John. 'Nawang (the cook) says you've got two cold, scared Sherpas. Maybe if you can persuade them to keep going until dawn, that might do the trick', he said.

Well, perhaps.

'Look, Ang Passang, let's just keep climbing until we catch up with the three ahead. We can discuss it with them.'

I tried everything. 'Take my jacket,' I said (I carried a spare one in my sack). 'If you get to the top? Yes, of course you can come to London.'

Hesitantly, they – we – moved on. It wasn't long before we caught up with the three climbers ahead; they were climbing without supplementary oxygen, and one was struggling with the cold.

But we didn't stop and discuss the advisability of our continued ascent, as I suggested we might; just wished them well and climbed on past.

We were now climbing at altitudes far higher than I had ever climbed before. Six, sometimes seven steps were as many as I could take in succession without stopping, leaning over my ice-axe and gasping for breath as if it were my last. And as we climbed higher so that number was reduced, and reduced again, until two steps, even one step, was all that I could manage.

But as with any challenge that at times might seem overwhelming, I knew that the important thing was to simply keep taking steps. If I could take one step, I could take another. And when things got really tough, when the negative part of my being threatened to fight into lead position, then I just had to play that trick in my mind and re-focus on the summit, visualize in my mind's eye what this effort was all about, and in so doing, re-summon the desire and in turn the energy to climb on – one more step, then another, slowly towards my goal.

Counting steps became something of a mantra, and when this failed me I called upon another mantra ever present in my mind. 'Mind you make it,' I'd whisper in my head. 'Mind you make it' – these the words written in an octogenarian's hand on the front page of my copy of *The Ascent of Everest*, the book that recounts the first ascent of Everest, by Sir Edmund Hillary and Sherpa Tenzing Norgay, in 1953. The words were inscribed by the leader of that historical expedition, and author of the book, Colonel John Hunt, later Lord Hunt, when I was privileged to meet him shortly before I left for Everest myself. A number of devices can be called upon when motivation is in need of a boost, but the belief and expectations of others is always a sure way to top up belief in one's self.

On the South East Ridge, dawn had broken. Looking up we could see the ridge sweep high above us and to the right, like a cast fishing line. It was at once breathtaking and daunting, for it still looked a hell of a way to climb.

Ψ

The snow lay deep on the ridge. Every step required a kick, and another kick, to secure a footing and ensure we didn't slide back through the soft snow to where we'd started. A light snow blew in our faces and the whole of Tibet to the north was one ominous snow cloud, nothing but an ethereal wall of grey. I worried that the cloud might blow over and our visibility would deteriorate; a nagging doubt – should we climb on? – haunted me every step of the way.

Focusing only on the difficulties of such a climb – the breathlessness, the pain, the anxiety – you might be forgiven for asking, why bother? But there were ample rewards. First there was the feeling that I was pushing myself to the absolute limit; that I was discovering mental and physical capabilities that I didn't know I had. That in itself was reward enough, but then there was the added bonus that the pushing of mental and physical boundaries strengthened my resolve for events that might prove testing in the future. I survived that, so I can put up with this!

Then there was the rare privilege of moving slowly through the highest wilderness in the world, without sight of another human being. There were Ang Passang and Kami Tchering, of course; but the three figures below us had dropped from view. The footsteps we kicked were into fresh, virgin snow. And when we took pause between the gasps for breath, and stood still, just for a moment, the panorama to the west was of one Himalayan peak stacked up behind another, and another, like the view from an aeroplane. There wasn't a person – or sign of a person – in sight.

Such an experience of solitude in this vast and inspiring landscape was in no way diminished because of the presence of Ang Passang and Kami Tchering. In fact, the opposite – which brings me to my final and most lasting reward.

Somewhere on the South East Ridge Ang Passang and Kami Tchering decided that they wanted to climb to the summit just as badly as I did. They didn't tell me this; I didn't try to extricate it from them in conversation. It was just implicitly understood from their gait, from the way they held themselves, and from the way they continued moving slowly, but positively, in an upward direction.

There was another thing implicitly understood as well: at such extreme altitude it was far too dangerous to leave anybody on their own, which meant that all three of us would make it to the summit, or none at all. This, I believe, was our strength.

Working together as a tightly knit team of three, we were to enjoy very real practical advantages. We could take it in turns to lead and kick bucket steps in the snow for those who followed, for example, thus sharing the load. But far, far more important, and memorable, was the psychological influence each one of us exerted on the other. Because it was all of us or none of us, the other two people's progress was equally as important as one's own. We cared for the others as much as we did for ourselves.

I mentioned before that I couldn't possibly have climbed Everest without the Sherpas. Looking back, their presence was crucial from the start. Early on their optimism and enthusiasm girded me on, gave me confidence. Then, after their change of heart, I was lost – until for reasons of their own they turned about and returned to Camp 2, and gave me hope once more. They were the company that gave me the courage to climb again to the South Col. And now, on this final push, their presence was my inspiration. When I lagged behind, a quick glance at the two figures ahead would draw me along, because I didn't want to let the two of them down, and I didn't want to let myself down either. My memory of our climbing the higher reaches of the South East Ridge is of the three of us acting as a single entity, joined as if tethered by an invisible rope.

After ten hours or so of climbing we finally stepped onto the South Summit and were able to look along the final ridge towards Hillary's Step, in the knowledge that just beyond that was the summit. The view took me completely by surprise. I couldn't say how many pictures I had seen of this summit ridge – plenty, for sure. I expected it – as indeed it was – to be rocky with a great snowy cornice, like a wave, beaten into shape by the prevailing westerly winds. But nothing had prepared me for its degree of exposure. To the left the ridge falls away abruptly, 2,000m into Nepal; and to the right, over 3,000m into Tibet.

'You go first, Kami Tchering,' I said.

'No, you can go.'

'No, you.'

Kami Tchering led, climbing down a little gully and onto the ridge, and I followed, Ang Passang close on my heels; and slowly we inched our way along a precariously thin line that lies between the precipitous rock and the fragile wave of snow. I checked, and re-checked, every placement of my boot before daring to commit my weight to it, conscious that a slip here would be my last.

Ahead lay what we knew to be the very last obstacle on the mountain: Hillary's Step, a sharp rise in the rock of some 12 metres, with an awkward, steeply sloping mantel and a void below wiser not to focus upon; named, of course, after Sir Edmund Hillary who, with Sherpa Tenzing Norgay, was the first to walk this path.

Inelegantly I grasped the rock and pulled, rammed, jostled and finally heaved my body onto the mantel and from there, planted my ice-axe into a snowy shelf an arm's reach above my head and, in an adrenalin-fired burst, scurried to the top.

It was all but over now. Ahead of us the ridge, snow-covered, was broader than before, more gently inclined, and the only challenge that lay ahead was to keep walking. For the first time I felt complete certainty that we would make it to the top. There were no obstacles ahead; the weather still held fair. It didn't matter what Bracknell said; we would make it.

Half an hour or so and there ahead of us was the summit, the mountain falling away on all sides. The three of us, climbing one behind the other, huddled into a little cluster and together stepped on top of the world.

It was a moment of intense personal pleasure. The cloud cleared and revealed a view across the Tibetan plateau that stretched seemingly forever: to China and Mongolia, no doubt. And looking down from this lofty eagle's nest I could see below us, on the northern side, the strip of lateral moraine alongside the East Rongbuk Glacier, where, almost four years before, we had pitched our advanced base camp; and, across the glacier, the first step of the North East Ridge, Bill's Buttress, where I had first donned harness, boots and crampons, where my Everest story began. To look down upon it was to know it intimately, like an old friend.

But then there were my new friends, too. Refocusing on the scene immediately around me, there was Ang Passang, radio in hand, and Kami Tchering, both bursting with joy. 'Summit, summit, summit!' they cried. 'We make summit!' Both Sherpas had been high on Everest before, but neither had made it to the top.

I knew then, as I know now, that to have stood on that highest point on Earth alone would have been seen as a far greater accomplishment; I would have been granted a far greater accolade. But the fact is I couldn't have done it without Ang Passang and Kami Tchering, and even had I been able, I wouldn't have swapped the pleasure of seeing the joy on their faces for all the accolades in the world. It is the memory of their summit jubilance that is the sweetest of all my memories on Everest.

REFLECTIONS

Reflecting back on our time on Everest my memory often highlights short episodes – snapshots in the mind – when four of us, even six of us, were squeezed into a mountain tent designed for two, perched at a precariously jaunty angle on the icy slopes of the Lhotse Face or else on the high, windswept plateau of the South Col. The wind howled eerily and all the while I was acutely aware that we were on the very frontier of where human beings can survive. At such altitudes we were far beyond the reach of any help. We were on our own: a small, tightly knit team of people working together, whose success or failure depended entirely on our own actions and no-one else's.

During these times my thoughts didn't turn to the usual superficialities that can so easily crowd our minds in our status-conscious, mercantile society. I didn't think about the clothes my companions wore, for example (they were anyway the same tired, smelly fleece and down as my own – we hadn't washed in three weeks!). I didn't think about the cars they drove or the houses in which they resided, both out of view and out of mind. Nor did I think of the jobs they held down at home. We had doctors on board, ex-servicemen, a plumber and an out-of-work reporter, just as examples. None of these things that might usually shape our lives, and for which we might strive so doggedly, even entered my consciousness. The mountains are like that; they strip you absolutely bare.

What did pass through my mind – cold and cramped in that tent-for-two – was whether my companions pulled their weight and contributed to the end-goal, or left the work to others. Whether they energized me or sapped the life from my bones. Whether they inspired or demoralized. Whether, in short, they had their heart in what they were doing.

And these questions I had to turn on myself as well, for each one of us was expected to be a contributor to the team, helping and supporting others, as well as relying upon and being inspired by others.

It is these things – governed by the head and the heart, the very core of our beings – that matter when you are a part of an expedition with eyes set on the summit of Everest. And it is these things that matter when you are a player in any team, whether that is a family, a sports team, or a corporation.

Ψ

All of us have it within us to be positive contributors to a team's efforts. The question is, how do we motivate ourselves and others to fulfil the potential within us and perform to our absolute best?

First, a vision. Just as an individual needs to know exactly what he or she wants to achieve, so does a team. Otherwise how do players in the team know in which direction to throw their energies? Where do they start?

On Everest the vision was crystal-clear. It was also simple. Each morning we had only to look up and know exactly where it was that we were heading.

In our domestic and corporate lives, however, things aren't always so clearly defined. We might have several Everests to climb, each calling upon our limited time. Sometimes one Everest might conflict with another. It's harder. Nonetheless, at any one point in time, it's crucial that every effort should be made to ensure absolute clarity about what it is we want to achieve, even if only in the short term, or else accept the fact that we don't know and lie fallow for a while. It isn't sufficient for the

CEO of a company to say, for instance, that the company's aim is to increase sales, or to be the best in its sector in the world. What does this mean? What do employees of that company have to aim for? A vision has to be specific. It has to be, for example, to increase sales by so many thousands of pounds within a specific time frame, or to create a new, clearly defined product, again within a time frame. Something clear and tangible and understandable; and something that can be celebrated when achieved.

And if that vision is on a grand scale, something that is attainable only after years of dedication, then it must be broken down into manageable chunks, achievements on a scale that people can relate to in the short-to-medium term and be congratulated for on the journey: Camps 1, 2, 3 and 4 on the ascent to the summit.

A word of warning, though: one danger that every leader of a team must be aware of is just how easily a vision, however clearly defined at the start, can become a little blurred around the edges in people's minds, or even forgotten. Once when visiting a company I paused to ask an employee, busily processing a pile of papers stacked high in her in-tray: 'What is this for? Have you any idea why you're working like this?' She answered, 'I haven't a clue; I just know I've got to clear this lot by the close of 5.00 p.m.' On further discussion it became clear, not entirely to my surprise, that she was totally disenchanted with her work; that she felt disconnected from her employers and, but for the money, she didn't see the point of coming in to work.

On Everest, it might seem at face value that every member of the team knew exactly why they were on the mountain and what it was they were to achieve. But look a little closer and there were some barriers between various members of the group that might have grown and become insurmountable had we not been aware of them and acted with everybody's best interests at heart.

To start, we weren't so much one unified team as two teams enveloped under the banner of one expedition. There were those of us from Britain (ten climbers and a support team of four), and a second team of eight, the Sherpas, who we didn't meet until we arrived in Kathmandu.

It would have been difficult to question the motivation of the British contingent, at least at the start: none was paid and each virtually fought for the chance to go to Everest. But what about the Sherpas? Did they want to climb to the top? Or support others to the top? Or was it only for a salaried job that they were there?

It is my belief that without repeated reinforcement of the vision and a reassurance that everyone was a valued contributor to the endgame, the Sherpas would have done a perfectly good job, collected their salaries and gone home. What they wouldn't have done necessarily is to go the extra mile, perform, to use an old-fashioned phrase, beyond the call of duty, and excel in the way that they did.

I am thinking particularly of the time that the Sherpas and I were at Camp 2 after having run from the storm on the South Col. Up until this episode the Sherpas were always optimistic that we would climb to the summit, but after our U-turn on the South Col it seemed they had taken a U-turn in their minds as well. 'Please don't go home', I said, 'We need you here. Come back up the mountain when you're rested.' I didn't appreciate the importance of these words at the time, but on reflection I think they might at least have been a factor in their decision to climb back up to the camp, prepared for another go.

Another thing: the message was clear only because I talked to the Sherpas face to face; the impact would have been considerably diluted if I had resorted to the radio. In the workplace e-mails, faxes and memos all serve a purpose, but they're impersonal and can easily be ignored. What counts is communication person to person – namely talking – and not just once, but regularly to reinforce the message.

Communication takes two, though, and what if the other party isn't prepared to listen? Looking back I don't believe our team of Britons and Sherpas would have functioned effectively had there not been a good dollop of basic human respect. The joy was that to respect the Sherpas was so effortless. As a group they are always ready to smile through adversity. And importantly, on Everest, they are competent, cautious and knowledgeable; they know the mountain better than anyone.

In truth it would have been difficult *not* to respect the Sherpas – although with a stretch of the imagination it's just about possible to envisage a situation in which our team from Britain might have viewed the Sherpas as a support team only there to assist in the carrying of loads. After all, money changed hands for this service. Had this been the case, had the Sherpas not been valued as an integral part of the climbing team, then my high point on Everest would have fallen a long way short of the summit.

Ang Passang, Kami Tchering and Tcheri Zhambu made it a pleasure for us to respect them, but we live in a world in which we know that the gift of respect isn't always so easy to give. In building effective teams, though, it is the job of the leader to approach others with an open heart, with intent to respect every individual – however menial their task – not just because this is decent human behaviour but because what we give we get back, and a group of people operating in an environment of mutual respect is going to be very much more successful than one that doesn't.

The same thing can be said for trust, that delicate relationship between people in which one knows the other will honour his or her word and have both their best interests at heart – something that bonds individuals yet so easily can be destroyed.

Trust takes time to build, and strengthens through experiences in which people have opportunity to prove their worth. On a mountain, trust is everything; a climber trusts his or her life to another clipped on the same rope. But in the workplace, too, it is essential if a team is to work effectively, with each member carrying a fair share of the load. How else can you appoint tasks to others and know they will be done? How else can you move forward towards a common goal?

Ψ

An integral part of trust is, of course, honesty – by which I don't mean simply the absence of lies but a commitment to share with others information that will affect the whole team. It isn't always easy. I remember one incident on Everest, shortly before the Sherpas and I retraced our steps back up to the South Col, when they were ready and expectant to go and I simply couldn't summon the energy to move. I could barely carry myself to their tent to deliver the pathetic news. Yet I couldn't leave this task to a messenger, tempting as it might have been. I knew the Sherpas would be disappointed in me and I didn't want that; but my consolation was that in delivering bad as well as good news they would at least know that I was striving to be open with them.

It worked the other way, too. If the Sherpas had any failing it was that in their generosity they wanted always to please, and that meant that sometimes they told you what they thought you might like to hear and not what they believed to be the truth. On occasions this approached the ridiculous. Sitting at the Base Camp I'd ask them, 'Do you think we could summit by the end of the week?' 'Yes! Yes!' they'd answer with enthusiasm, knowing that my confidence could do with a boost. 'No!' I cried, 'we haven't yet established our first camp!'

Imagine how damaging this could be in a company. Somebody might ask a colleague how things are progressing only to receive a positive reply because he or she wants to give a good impression. Then, too late, it's discovered that this colleague has failed to declare a problem that's been allowed to fester and grow out of control, unchecked.

A culture of honesty in which people are encouraged to declare mistakes as readily as positive performances – and quickly – is critical if a team is to progress expediently, and, more crucially, not invite upon itself a nosedive to self-destruction. And for this to have any hope of working there must also be a culture free from fear – a culture in which people are congratulated for spotting problems early, even if they are their own, so that the problems can be dealt with immediately and the team be allowed to move on.

There was one more important factor that I believe contributed to our success on Everest, and that was belief – not just belief in one's self, but also the belief of others. Fast-tracking a few years, I found myself one day at the airport in Kathmandu, just having completed a trek in the Everest region. Moving in the direction of the departure lounge my eyes settled on a Sherpa, comfortably plump of figure and dressed in a grey suit. I caught his eye but didn't recognize him at first, until he smiled. It was Chhwang, the sirdar who on my first trip to Everest had so generously tipped open his rucksack and handed over his mountain boots and crampons, harness and ice-axe, so that I might climb to my self-appointed 'summit' atop Bill's Buttress on the North East Ridge.

Chhwang had moved on in the intervening years – he was managing director of a trekking company (hence the rounded belly and suit) – but back on that first expedition he had opened a door for me that quite literally changed my life. For it wasn't only his climbing kit that he had given me on that occasion, but an unspoken belief. Chhwang exuded an attitude that was entirely positive: if a stranger from the other side of the world – a novice at that – wants to climb onto Everest's North East Ridge, why not? He didn't have any doubt that I could do it. His belief in me propped up a belief in myself (one that might easily have wavered in his absence) so that I had the confidence to climb Bill's Buttress, and in so doing, discover a passion that was to lead to my climbing Everest, and the Seven Summits, and to learn from these experiences lessons that have led to the writing of this book.

Chhwang's attitude was reflected in that of Ang Passang's and Kami Tchering's four years on. It was easy for me to believe in them: they were the experts. But I'll always thank them for believing that I could climb that mountain. As indeed I will thank John for his belief in the Sherpas and me on that dreadful night of uncertainty on the South Col. 'I think you'll be OK,' he said – that was all we needed.

John's role as leader of the expedition was exemplary that night. To lead an expedition wasn't anything that was new to him; he had led a number of Himalayan climbs before. However, he had led none where he wasn't up there at the front, able to take action if needed. None where he had to manage his own disappointment, knowing his actions had saved Harry's life but also cost him his own chance of climbing Everest. And none where he was in a position to hand over responsibility to three Sherpas and me, a relative newcomer to the game, his student, in the knowledge that if we failed to return, he would be the one left to agonize over how things might have been very different.

In short, that night John found the courage to hand over the reins – not just anywhere, but on the biggest mountain in the world. That takes trust. That takes a mutual respect between members of the team – and an openness and honesty, too. The lines of communication were open to transmit and receive throughout the making of John's brave decision.

Perhaps this is the mark of an exemplary leader; that he or she is prepared to hand over responsibility to other members of the team. People thrive on responsibility, after all. It allows us to feel valued, to stretch ourselves, improve performance, be fulfilled.

There is no doubt there are risks in this approach, which is why so many people shy away from it. Nonetheless, I would argue that even if mistakes are made, this approach is far more productive than the alternative. If a leader is over-controlling and reluctant to hand over any responsibility, the result is a stifled, demotivated workforce that simply 'gets the job done' (if you're lucky). There is no room for self-expression, no room for stretching one's abilities or going the extra mile. No room for excellence.

Far better then to allow people to make a few mistakes and view these as lessons on the road to progress.

To conclude: If leadership is, in part, making decisions that influence the outcome of the team's efforts, then on Everest there was a fluidity that allowed different people to lead depending on the circumstances. Whoever was last at a particular camp, for example, would make decisions on resupplies; Harry made decisions on his solo oxygen-less ascent; and the Sherpas and I made decisions high on Everest on that summit day.

And if leadership is also to inspire and support other members of the team in order to progress positively towards a common goal, then this, too, was a role taken on by different players at different times. The Sherpas were unfailing in their role as leaders in this regard; their optimism fuelled my confidence from start to finish. But on the odd occasion when their resolve wavered, I stepped in. Then mine wavered, and they stepped in. That is the way of things: sometimes one individual feels the stronger; at other times, another. In isolation, none of us would have made it to the top of Everest; but with a team it was an achievement won and celebrated.

Trusting to Teamwork 2

Even the most egocentric, dynamic, inspired and potent manager can't do it all alone – although to read much business journalism, you wouldn't think so. The articles and the PROs laud the apparently lone management summiteers. The latter in real life have no do-it-myself option. Like any manager, they have to work with and through other people. The better the people, and the more effective the working relationships, vertical and horizontal alike, the stronger and more enduring will be the achievement.

The combined efforts and internal dynamics of the team are as crucial in management as on Everest. What Rebecca describes as 'the joy of working together' should apply equally; and so should 'the collective power of a team of people'. As noted in my previous chapter, psychologists teach that several brains in real-time combination are always more powerful than a single brain – no matter how brilliant. Without truly belonging to her team, Rebecca would never have reached that highest of all summits.

She depended vitally on the other team members, true. Yet the first lesson of teamwork, as she writes, is to shun 'dependency'. Rather, 'interdependence' holds the key. You rely on others and draw on their strengths. They in turn rely on and draw strengths from you – and from the other team-mates. The big (and common) mistake is to ignore this mutuality. You can't simply allot people to various posts and assume that this constitutes a team; any more than you can join two people in matrimony and assume that this constitutes a happy marriage. Working upwards from subservient group to proactive team is one of management's most demanding and satisfying tasks.

My previous chapter described how, more and more, companies are recognizing team-power by 'project management', delegating mountainous challenges to purpose-built teams. In many high-profile cases, these groupings (sometimes going under the name of 'skunk works', a phrase which graphically describes their isolation and independence), have vastly exceeded even high expectations. That's in large part because project management beats bureaucracy and frees up enterprise. But nothing can be taken for granted in teamwork. Team leaders have to master three always difficult tasks:

- Remove the barriers between individuals and achieve unity of purpose.

- Develop and sustain the Three Graces of teamwork – Trust, Respect and Honesty.

- Make the impossible possible – as in the exceeded expectations mentioned above.

Meet those needs and you develop real teamwork – and, even more important, since it is the foundation of effective action, you create 'teamthink'. There's a mighty gulf between 'groupthink' and 'teamthink'. In the former, individual ideas are discouraged, even suppressed, for the sake of a consensus often imposed from the top down. All or some of the individuals may develop better ideas than the groupthink bandwagon. But groupthink swamps individual faculties by the pressures of conformity, which often enshrines prejudice and the most dangerous and pervasive phenomenon of all: nonthink.

In contrast, teamthink is the sum of individual ideas openly aired and discussed. Team meetings under this dispensation aren't exercises in boosting morale, but the only practicable way of achieving the team purpose. Every team member has their own clearly designated function and role, but everybody understands the functions and roles of everybody else. Quite naturally, the lead in a particular instance is taken by whoever has the relevant authority of expertise. Agreement is reached, not by adversarial debate, but by communal discussion.

The 'human resources' experts employed by great companies are fully aware of the sovereign importance of teamwork. Few management specialists are more knowledgeable; they should be, for few managers attend or arrange more conferences and courses. Management by lip-service, however, is nowhere more prevalent than in 'HR'. The rot, as it usually does, starts at the top, the executive leadership. Annual reports commonly boast that 'people are our most important asset' when said assets are often treated in ways that would have any self-respecting machine seizing up in seconds.

That happens to people, too. Seizure, though, can't be afforded at a time when, thanks to profound changes in people themselves, in technology and in employment, people have become our 'most important everything'. Not only are individual contributions the building blocks of the twenty-first century enterprise. It's the way in which individual talents are combined that is decisive. Yet 'teams' and 'teamwork' are prime areas of HR management by lip-service. In hard practice, companies still rely on hierarchy and habit (not forgetting sticks and carrots) to keep individuals in line.

Ψ

An American musical comedy, *How to Succeed in Business Without Really Trying*, featured the lyric, 'I do it the company way – the company way is by me OK'. It would not be sung today. The words embody degrees of loyalty and obedience (not to say servility) that once cemented organizations and controlled careers for working lifetimes. Today education and upbringing are creating more individualistic personalities and wants. Changes in life patterns and in digital awareness have reinforced the trend and are reflected in work patterns.

The change in people coincides with the changes in employment in 'the knowledge economy'. Information technology has played a decisive role in this rise, but many other and diverse skills have also become essential. These portable skills act as a kind of passport for knowledge workers, who travel from job to job, organization to organization, and often from paid full-time employment to contractual status; and who perhaps work for several employers simultaneously.

The still-gathering trend towards outsourcing manufacture, services and processes further weakens a single management's power to control how people do their work. So, too, does the proliferation of joint ventures. These take staff into new situations where the lines of authority are blurred, but where responsibility resides clearly at the sharp end. As more jobs are contracted out, too, more of the remaining employees act increasingly in a contractor or consultancy mode.

Organizations, like it or not, are changing to accommodate the resulting pressures. Hence phenomena like 'hot-desking', 'telecommuting', 'flexitime', the 'skunk works' mentioned earlier, 'hot groups', 'self-managed teams' and so on. All take the individual, laptop and PDA at the ready, away from the familiar 9–5, office-based, centralized routine; and away, too, from the static, solid management structures that the routine enshrined. Instead, the structure is loosely built from large numbers of teams, some permanent, others constantly changing personnel and tasks until eventual dissolution – when the tasks are complete.

There's no problem in fitting such people into teams, because you naturally fit the teams to the people. The team is a living being, an organism that follows a logic of its own in forming relationships and conducting operations. The analogy is not, as in traditional management, with the military, but with team sports, orchestras and jazz combos – especially the latter, with their freewheeling solos alternating with ensembles, all built on a unifying theme.

Since the pioneering work of Meredith Belbin, it's been accepted that business teams, like athletes and musicians, need a combination, not only of professional talents, but also of personal attributes. His original list, which needs little if any further explanation, comprised:

- Coordinator

- Ideas person

- Critic

- Implementer

- External contact

- Inspector

- Team-builder.

You don't need seven different people: doubling or trebling up are allowed. But you do need to ensure that all seven roles are performed by somebody. Note the absence of 'leader'. Note, too, the difficulty of deciding which of these seven roles best fits the leader concept. Note, also, that traditional leaders will find good (and bad) reasons why they need to take all seven roles unto themselves. There is an element of truth in this, however. The leader needs to pay active personal attention to all of the Belbin roles. But the leader's responsibility here is to manage the role-holders, not to usurp their tasks.

Like most of management, though, teamwork has moved on over the post-war period, becoming more complex and less self-evident. The Belbin Seven have been expanded by their creator to Nine. Only two are identical (Coordinator and Implementer), and several require considerable explanation:

Role	Attributes
Plant	Creative, imaginative, unorthodox. Solves difficult problems.
Resource investigator	Extrovert, enthusiastic, communicative. Explores opportunities, develops contacts.
Coordinator	Mature, confident, a good chairperson. Clarifies goals, promotes decision-making, delegates well.
Shaper	Challenging, dynamic, thrives on pressure. Has the drive and courage to overcome obstacles.
Monitor evaluator	Sober, strategic, discerning. Sees all options, judges accurately.
Teamworker	Cooperative, mild, perceptive, diplomatic. Listens, builds, averts friction, calms the waters.
Implementer	Disciplined, reliable, conservative, efficient. Turns ideas into practical actions.
Completer	Painstaking, conscientious, anxious. Searches out errors and omissions, delivers on time.
Specialist	Single-minded, self-starting, dedicated. Provides knowledge and skills in short supply.
	Source: Sue Clemenson (*Manager's Handbook*, ed. Robert Heller: Dorling Kindersley 2002)

The immediate reaction to Belbin Mark II has to be WOW! Have nine such paragons ever been gathered under one roof, let alone in one team? The Nine have to be considered as aspirations, as guides to training and development, as benchmarks against which reality can be measured and missing pieces identified. All that must be among the indispensable roles of the team leader, who is certainly going to require a formidable number of the Nine qualities and attributes on his or her own account.

Leadership is discussed more fully in the next chapter. But it also has a critical role in the 'self-managed teams' mentioned above. The concept hinges on establishing clear, but shared responsibilities and on having an equally clear, unambiguous answer to the essential question, 'who's in charge here?' The difference from traditional management is that the leader, while still responsible for the performance of the team as a whole, is also responsible to the team for the effective performance of his or her own role.

Ψ

The resulting issues won't be resolved just by HR nostrums. Take the basic matter of reward: maintaining self-managed teams, in office tasks and cellular manufacturing, etc., logically suggests rewarding team members partly for the collective work provided by them all, partly for individual contributions. This fruitful idea has been around a long time (since the Middle Ages, as it happens), but is more a practical factor than a motivational force. Winning better outcomes from the combined endeavours of free spirits demands deeper solutions.

In fact, brain-workers have never been especially susceptible to traditional management – witness the persistent failure of efforts to 'manage' research and development, which stubbornly refuses to obey the rules of other activities. Now the difficulty has spread throughout organizations. The challenge of managing people who have their own important, individual agendas, and aligning the latter with the corporate purpose, affects management behaviour everywhere. The challenge cries out for the new teamwork – and can hardly be met without it.

The current great movement of management from rigidity to flexibility, and from dictation to responsiveness, conflicts with hierarchy at every point. Most firms are still organized on pyramid principles, which don't encourage individualism and rule-breaking, but very much encourage groupthink and making rules.

The model is basically military. Having everybody knowing their place and staying there greatly simplifies formal communication. But management research has shown that much of this communication is ineffective, and that, anyway, most effective communicating was always informal, even before e-mail, intranets and IT revolutionized interaction. The task is to make ample room in the system and the job specifications for the high-powered, purposeful informality so encouraged by the Web.

A precondition for fulfilling this task is radical departure from the pyramid – in particular, transition from order-and-obey (or command and control) to MCC (management by consent and consensus). The great majority of managers, in fact, recognize the MCC relationship. They earnestly believe, according to one study, that the quality of decisions and their implementation is significantly improved by involving the widest possible number in the decision process.

However (and very sadly), an equally large body of managers in the same survey admitted that they fail to consult or even communicate with their people before decisions are taken. Unless this disconnect is healed, the employee dissatisfaction that breeds under-performance will continue. The easy excuse for sticking to the old ways and shunning the new is that the benefits of flexible teamwork are hard to quantify, while those of old-style management are easily measured. Financial targets for sales and profits may actually be meaningless, but they sound meaningful, and are easily linked with reward systems by widespread devices such as commissions and bonuses.

In contrast, tolerating and humouring eccentrics, oddballs and exceptions, while now recognized as a sign, even cause of rude corporate health, is not measurable, either in itself or its benefits. Acceptance of this fact (and of the oddballs) demands flexibility from managers and co-workers alike. Tolerance can be reinforced by involving superiors, peers and subordinates in appraisals, and scoring performance in a more or less scientific manner. But this approach, while useful, can't be the only measure.

For one rigid, inescapable condition carries over from the old management to the new – the requirement for excellent performance, for desired outcomes, which is the proper purpose and acid test of any organization. What does performance mean, though? In the bygone era when conglomerates were kings, performance was reduced to sets of financial digits. But crucial matters such as innovation and creativity, quality and value, speed to market and teamwork, customer service and leadership cannot fit into the financial straitjacket. Various metrics are required for all the different outcomes, but three questions apply generally:

- What is the task that this team has accepted?

- What input and output criteria have been agreed?

- Using those criteria, what has been achieved?

There's an obvious fit between the outcomes approach to measurement and the control of semi-detached workers who are vital to the organization, but have opted for a contractual relationship. This differs little in nature and measurement needs from contracts negotiated with outsiders (including suppliers of outsourced services and manufacture). But the method is also widely applicable internally. Managements have to find ways of working with people who are not simply given orders, but contribute largely to determining what work they should do, and how it will be done.

Ψ

The transition is full of hope. New Age management, with its insistence on the outcome, not the method; on the primacy of the individual as team member; and on human values is much more complex and demanding. It is also (another paradox) more productive. According to Bronwyn Fryer, writing in the *Harvard Business Review*, companies that focus on 'amplifying positive attributes such as loyalty, resilience, trustworthiness, humility and compassion ... perform better, financially and otherwise'.

It should go without saying that these attributes must be reciprocal. Trust cannot be a one-way street. The obstacles to better outcomes are mostly not 'hard' and technical, but 'soft' and human – like trust. The very specific issues of motivating and measuring performance inside new, broad philosophies of management can only be tackled through applying those very philosophies. These in turn cannot operate without sweeping changes in the relationship between management and all subordinates, from top to bottom of the enterprise.

The true team leader doesn't follow old models and modes at all. He or she concentrates, not on dominating a consensus, but on ensuring that one is reached. It's messy, especially when compared with the traditional military mode, which infects teamwork, too. 'Team briefings', for example, are a well-known military method for sharing knowledge about strategy, plans and other developments.

The cascade principle used is common in civilian use: the chief executive briefs the senior management, who disperse to brief their 'reports', who disperse to brief their teams, and so on. But is this top-down approach the best way to motivate and mobilize? More, are these genuine teams? More likely, they are little more than units, whose involuntary members share neither a common purpose nor any significant say over how the unit goes about its business. There is no togetherness.

In real life, true teams, of course, can be riven by hatreds and jealousies. Calling somebody a team leader doesn't cure his or her faults, or guarantee a positive and constructive relationship with associates. The truth is that 'team' is a word of much vagueness. The best the dictionary can do (after 'two or more beasts harnessed together') is 'a set of persons working together'. That settles nothing. How many people make a set? The answer can extend from those two or more beasts to the hundreds who may be needed for a crash project.

The important words are 'working together'. That means far more than 'working alongside': it means that interdependence of which Rebecca writes. You can't do your work without the others, and *vice versa*. Moreover, common purpose is essential. Apart from other considerations (like pointing everybody in the same direction), the purpose defines the nature of the team, and thus of its work.

There's a world of difference, and many corporate layers, between an executive team and a 'hot group'. The first isn't an ad hoc body, but a more or less permanent group of senior managers who share the responsibility for decisions and individually supervise certain operations. The second is distinguished by its high degree of autonomy and innovatory purpose. Unlike a project team, which is given a defined task, these groups make up their tasks and their methods as they go along. They have some affinity with task forces, which, however, exist to solve problems – ranging from defects on the production line to a breakdown in a nationwide marketing channel.

There are cross-functional teams, business unit teams, formal support teams (like finance departments or IT or HR), change teams, and so on. Plainly, the nature and *modus operandi* of these teams must vary with the task, the leadership and the numbers. Numbers matter: Anthony Jay, who went on to co-write the brilliant political satire, *Yes Minister*, created a considerable stir in the early Seventies with a book that made much of the 'hunting group' and its headcount.

According to *Corporation Man*, the early historical experience of man the hunter set an atavistic limit on numbers, which determines the boundaries of effectiveness to this day. It is true that a large team will naturally split into sub-teams of manageable size. But their loyalties will be to the broader team leader as well as their own smaller section. It's this community of interest that ultimately defines a team, establishes its effectiveness and enables it to pass some tough tests.

- Do the team members know and like each other and respect their capabilities?

- Do they feel the same positive way about their leader?

- Has the latter shared the team's purpose and its goals with all its members?

- Does the leader keep everybody up-to-date with progress against goals and all matters relevant to the success of the team?

- Do team members have a say in the selection of new recruits and the promotion of existing members?

- Is the reward system seen as fair – and linked to team as well as individual success?

- Do members help to develop stretching goals?

- Are contributions to team success formally recognized and informally celebrated?

- Are meetings of all kinds welcomed, enjoyed and thought constructive?

- Is everybody encouraged to produce and report on new ideas?

This list of questions, all demanding the answer YES, is by no means exhaustive, but it won't be exhausting, either, if friendship and enthusiasm are sustained. They won't be unless the team leader and his or her superiors choose to live by the same statement from these three alternatives:

1   I do not trust this person/team to do a proper job, and will replace them as soon as possible.

2   I do not trust this person/team to do a proper job, but control them tightly to ensure that they do.

3   I trust this person/team to do a proper job, and will let them get on with it in their own way.

Any sensible person plumps for the third alternative, whether in a factory or an office – or on a mountain. Yet the majority of managers, perfectly sensible in other ways, gravitate towards the second. If the person is not competent to do the job, why are they still in the position? If they are competent, though, why are you not allowing them to demonstrate that competence? The whole concept of the team hinges on people with the ability and authority to do their work to excellent standards – helping to create an enterprise that is truly a productive team of self-fulfilling teams.

Work is not, of course, play. But a successful team sets about its work in the same spirit as the little girl approached by the researchers Peter and Iona Opie when studying children's play. 'What are you playing at?', they asked. 'I'm not playing', she replied, 'This is what I do'. A good team isn't 'working', but living and loving and doing its work.

- Create a **team vision** that is clear, tangible and understandable – and can be celebrated when achieved.

- Break down the task into **manageable chunks** to which people can relate in the short to medium term.

- Draw strength from and rely upon **other team members**, while supporting and inspiring them in turn.

- Do the talking in **face to face communication**, not just once, but over and over to reinforce the message.

- Encourage people to **declare mistakes** as readily as they hail positive performances – frankly and quickly.

- **Remove** the **barriers** between people; develop and sustain trust, respect and honesty; make the impossible possible.

- **Fit** the **team to** the **people**, not the people to the team.

- Join the **big switch** from order-and-obey (or command and control) **to MCC** (management by consent and consensus).

- **Ask** repeatedly, **how has this team performed** against its agreed objectives and its input and output criteria?

- **Strive to create** an enterprise that is truly **a highly productive team** of self-fulfilling teams.

Finding True Leadership 1

MOUNT ELBRUS, 5,642m (18,510ft)

Mont Blanc is sometimes mistakenly thought of as the highest peak in Europe, but in fact, Mount Elbrus in the Caucasus range, between the Black and the Caspian Seas, is just short of 1,000m higher. The Caucasus mark the delineation between Europe to the north and Asia to the south, and Elbrus is on the northern side, at the southern edge of Russia. It was off limits to most climbers until the mid 1980s when perestroika and glasnost allowed unrestricted access through the former USSR. A massive, extinct two-headed volcano, it is plastered with some 70 glaciers.

Everest climbed, I had a book to write, sponsorship obligations to fulfil and a life to get back onto some sort of an even keel. But come the spring of the following year, 1994, and my thoughts were once again in the hills. I had that promise to myself to keep: to climb the Seven Summits, the highest mountain on each of the seven continents.

With some degree of satisfaction I could reflect on the fact that of the Seven, three – including the biggest – I had already climbed. Yet I couldn't afford to be complacent. On the two most challenging of these three mountains – Denali and Everest – I had been a player in a team under the leadership of another, namely John. Now, if I was to move forward and climb the remaining four peaks, I could no longer depend on his guidance. I would have to grasp the challenge and organize each of the climbs myself. In business terms, I was moving off the shop floor into a position of management.

Given an ideal world, I would have hoped to climb one of the remaining mountains a year, even every two years, with time enough to explore the surrounding landscapes and cultures. But of course it isn't an ideal world and, just as in business, I had to work within the parameters of certain constraints, the most immediate of which were budget – and competition.

To secure sponsorship I would have to be the first British woman to climb the Seven Summits, and, annoyingly, there was another British woman – her name, Dr Ginette Harrison – who was ahead of the game. Ginette had climbed Everest the same year as me, but as well as Denali she had also climbed Aconcagua, the highest mountain in South America, which, at 6,960m (22,834ft), is the biggest challenge of the Seven after Everest.

I picked up the phone and called David Allen, UK Chairman of the courier company DHL, which had so brilliantly sponsored us on Everest, and put it to him that he might consider sponsoring me to climb the Seven Summits.

'Well,' he said gently, 'there won't be any money unless you're first.'

The news came as no surprise, really. It just meant that I had to abandon my romantic notion of climbing one mountain a year, or two years, and run! Naturally the first thing I had to do was to make a plan – and that plan had to be worked back from the end-goal, the last of the Seven Summits, which was to be Vinson in Antarctica.

Why was Vinson to be the last? Because of all the mountains, Vinson was the most season-dependent. Without an unlimited budget and a willingness to climb in the Antarctic winter, it was impossible for me, or Ginette, to approach the mountain until November – the beginning of the Antarctic summer – when Adventure Network International (ANI), the only flight operator in the region, scheduled its first flight from Punta Arenas in the southern tip of Chile, across the Southern Ocean, to the icy wastelands of Antarctica. I wanted to be on ANI's first flight and for Vinson to be the last of my Seven Summits, because Ginette couldn't better that – although she could of course equal it, which was the best that I could hope for. What this meant, though, was that in the months leading up to November I was to climb the three other remaining peaks, if, that is, I was to win the funding to climb them at all.

Of the three, neither Elbrus, the highest in Europe, nor Carstensz Pyramid, the highest in Australasia, posed a problem in terms of scheduling. Both could be climbed at any time in the summer months. The one problem was Aconcagua, the South American peak that Ginette had already climbed. Usually this is climbed in December, January or February (again in the southern hemisphere, these are the summer months). But if I left it until then I would fail to climb it before Vinson. So I had to take a chance; I had to schedule to climb it out of season in October, and pray the weather would be kind.

It was a new role for me to think in these terms. Ahead of me lay a marvellous adventure, but in order to ensure its success I had to drive the whole operation and work to deadlines and within budget. I had to organize transport, accommodation, permits, climbing kit and food and, most important, the people with whom I would climb.

Ψ

Elbrus was the first mountain on which I was the one responsible for selecting who would comprise the team. Mainly for reasons of cost I restricted the number of expedition members who were to travel from the UK to two – myself and one other. And that one other was to be great friend of mine, Fiona Gately. Fiona and I had known each other from university, for the best part of 15 years, but I chose the words 'expedition member' carefully, rather than 'climber' – because the latter Fiona certainly was not. Fiona had grown up in Hong Kong and not so much as walked on snow.

Why, if I wanted to succeed, would I choose her as a climbing companion? Many people asked me this question, and quite reasonably so. They supposed, as I supposed, that Fiona's progress on the mountain would determine mine – if she were to fail, I would fail. But I reckon I understood what it took to climb a high but otherwise straightforward mountain like Elbrus and answered the doubting Thomases: because Fiona's tough, she's unbelievably determined and she's up for an adventure. These seemed perfectly valid reasons for me to invite her along – aside from the obvious reason, of course, that we'd have a lot of fun.

It is often said that companies hire people for their skills and fire them for their personality, and on reflection I can see that, quite unintentionally, I turned this truism on its head. I invited Fiona along for her character and her wants and felt confident that given a couple of weeks scampering about on some moderate peaks in the Caucasus she would have time enough to acquire the requisite skills to climb Elbrus. Why not? After all, I too had started with no experience and yet passionately wanted to climb a mountain, not so very long ago.

For me it was a strange role reversal, though. On both Denali and Everest I had been a pupil, soaking up knowledge and gleaning what I could from other people. Now

Fiona was to be the pupil and I was to be a teacher – although not in the full meaning of the word.

I had decided early on that Fiona and I wouldn't climb Elbrus alone. Instead we would be accompanied by a Russian mathematician called Sergei, who, for much of the year lectured at St Petersburg University but who, like so many Russians, loved to escape to the hills.

Inviting Sergei along might have been perceived as cowardice in a way, for a part of the mountaineering ethos is to give the mountain a sporting chance, not to invite a helping hand who might offer an unfair advantage. But I simply couldn't resolve the alternative as anything other than foolhardy and irresponsible. Elbrus isn't technically difficult in the slightest, but it is high – 5,642m (18,510ft) – and for most of the climb we'd be moving roped together on one of a number of glaciers. I could just about envisage, should Fiona fall down a crevasse, that I might be able to help her out; but I had real problems imagining what would happen should I be the one to fall down a crevasse. Would Fiona, a diminutive 5'2" to my 5'10" and with no experience, be able to help me out?

We took the safe option. Sergei, who had climbed in the Caucasus a number of times, could act as our guide, and he could also teach Fiona the finer nuances of rope work and the ice-axe arrest. My role would be more one of encouragement – coach, if you like – making every effort to inspire in her a confidence and a manifest belief that she could do it, just as the Sherpas had offered the gift of belief to me.

I had a lot to learn in this role, though, as I was quickly to discover.

We couldn't have been climbing for more than a couple of days when Sergei and I spotted an attractive-looking gully to climb. For me, and certainly for Sergei, it fell within our parameter of experience – it was snow-filled, not too steeply angled. But Fiona had climbed for only two days in her life. She'd had opportunity to grow accustomed to her oversized plastic mountain boots and crampons, but not much else.

Sergei scampered up the gully and Fiona and I followed, roped together. We had only gone a few paces when, below me, Fiona cried, 'Don't leave me!' I felt a smile creep across my face, for it seemed only yesterday that I had cried the exact same words when John had first led me up a gully; yet a part of me was also angry with myself for causing Fiona anxiety.

It is perhaps at this point that I should take the trouble – as I should have done then, but failed – to describe some rules of climbing roped together. The whole point of climbing roped, of course, is that one climber can offer protection to another climber should he or she fall. There are many variables in the action called upon to offer such protection, depending on whether the climbers are on a glacier, a rock face or a ridge; but in a snowy gully such as we were climbing in the Caucasus, should one climber fall, the other would throw his or herself belly down in the snow, full body weight thrust down upon an ice-axe, which, spike into the snow, should break the fall. All very well, but reactions need to be speedy; and it's helpful if the climber below rather than the one in a higher position takes a tumble, else the falling climber builds up such momentum that he or she is likely to catapult the other off the mountainside.

Let's assume for a moment, though, that it is the lower climber (Fiona) who is to be protected. In this situation, the higher climber (namely, me) needs to be at a certain distance, say 10m, above the lower climber in order to have time (admittedly limited) to react if the lower climber falls. The rope that tethers the lower and higher climber also needs to be at a certain tension – not so tight that it tugs at the lower climber and restricts his or her movement, and not so loose that, should the lower climber fall, there's lots of slack in the rope to be taken up before the higher climber has a chance to break the fall (another situation where the falling climber builds up such dangerous speed that he or she might pull the other climber off the mountain).

So what did this all mean when Fiona cried, 'Don't leave me!'? It meant that it was difficult for me to be obliging and descend to where she was, and stay close to her, without compromising our safety.

'Well, just leave me alone then! Let me come up in my own time!' she cried, a perceptible quiver in her voice. Again, these were almost the exact same words I remember crying when I was first led up a gully, though this hardly offered any comfort. The fact is that I couldn't leave her on her own; conversely I wanted her to hurry up! The sun was climbing high in the sky and the risk of rock fall increasing with every passing second, but how could I explain this to her without shattering her already fragile nerves?

Fiona and I got to the top of the gully, and on safe ground Fiona sat down in the snow – a small heap of nervous exhaustion. All I could say is that I was very, very sorry.

The lesson, surely, is that I should have briefed Fiona properly *before* we climbed the gully. I should have spelt out to her the need to keep the rope between us at a certain length and tension, and the need to move without delay to reduce the risk of rock fall. Then, armed with this knowledge, she could have made a decision as to whether or not to climb, and, if affirmative, mentally prepared herself and minimized the risks accordingly.

I was lucky that Fiona was made of tough stuff and picked herself up and moved on; and I was lucky, too, that she forgave me this error of judgement – although only the next day it was her turn to act in a way that called upon some understanding from me. We were climbing a small peak, an easy peak – not very high and with no challenging obstacles whatsoever – when, just short of the summit, Fiona sat down on a rock and flatly refused to go on.

'But Fiona, it's only a ten minute scramble and we'll be at the top.'

It was to no avail. She wouldn't budge and so I left her sitting with Sergei and scrambled to the top myself, muttering under my breath in disbelief, 'If she can't climb this, how the hell is she going to climb Elbrus?'

It was as well that I had twenty minutes on my own – time enough to collect myself and rationalize my thoughts. Yes, I was disappointed with her; she surely could have climbed to this point. But the question I had to ask myself was whether or not she *wanted* to climb it. On Elbrus, I told myself, she'd perform, she'd put in the effort. And with that thought, I bit my lip and said nothing, knowing that the important thing was not to express any doubt in her commitment but rather to offer her the gift of belief that the Sherpas had so brilliantly given me.

It wasn't so difficult. My doubt subsided almost as quickly as it raised its ugly head. I had complete faith in Fiona's ability to climb the highest mountain in Europe, which, I'm pleased to say, she did. It was a slow old plod to the summit, but the sky was an intense, high-altitude blue and a carpet of cotton wool cloud stretched out to the horizon beneath our feet. 'That day on the summit was like living in a dream,' said Fiona – simple words, but ones that made it worthwhile.

REFLECTIONS

At the time it seemed a perfectly natural choice for me to invite Fiona along to Elbrus, despite her obvious lack of climbing experience. Her toughness and aspirations seemed far more important qualities for the job. Of course it would be madness to totally dismiss a lack of learning or skills in a number of professions – medicine and engineering, just as examples. And yet it's worth asking, are the requisite skills enough? Should we employ people only on the basis of their qualifications, even experience gained; or should we look, too, at how they will perform and what they will contribute in the future? The latter depends a great deal on energy, aspirations and wants – and can't be ignored.

Another thing to be ignored only at one's peril is the infinitesimally fine line that lies between an individual's confidence and loss of nerve. Fiona might justifiably have thrown in the ice-axe when I made such a poor judgement in that snowy gully. She didn't, but had she been only marginally less robust, I would have blown it.

Underneath the superficiality of our veneer the majority of us are really quite fragile creatures. Some might be more robust than others; but all of us can benefit from a series of positive accomplishments rather than needless disasters caused only because we are unprepared. On Elbrus it was my responsibility – miserably neglected – to prepare Fiona for that snowy gully, to brief her, to explain the safety mechanisms of climbing roped together, even to have led her up a gentler gully before embarking on one as daunting. In business it's the responsibility of a leader or coach to step into the shoes of his or her employees, just for a moment, and imagine what it must be like to be in a strange, new and perhaps intimidating environment, and to provide instruction and training accordingly, so that they can progress with confidence rather than a feeling of inadequacy.

I like the analogy of climbing roped together. The leader in the higher position keeps a watchful eye on his or her employee, ensuring the rope is neither too taut – too controlling – so there's no room for self-expression on the part of the employee, nor too slack so there's no fear that a slip will result in disaster. Climbing roped, both leader and employee reach the top together – or else they fail together. Looked at in this way, it is crucial to invest as much energy in developing your employees as it is in yourself.

Finding True Leadership 2

The first person that a leader must lead is him or herself. Rebecca discovered this governing truth when she moved on (as one should) to the next challenge. Completing the Seven Summits meant climbing four mountains in four corners of the world in five months – and doing so under the lash of competition: another Brit, Dr Ginette Harrison, was already ahead of the game. Rebecca had no choice but to deploy the five Ps of Leadership – PURPOSE, PLAN, PROGRESS, PEOPLE and PERFORMANCE – to accomplish this formidable task.

If you're to follow leaders, they and you had best know where the party is heading. That's PURPOSE. You won't get there without working out the route, the logistics, the equipment and the timetable. That's the PLAN. The latter will probably not work out as expected – so you must monitor developments and adapt the plan, even reverse it, as necessary. That's how you PROGRESS the project.

The success with which the first three Ps are deployed depends utterly on the fourth, the leader's interaction with the rest of the party. That's PEOPLE. And all the first four come to nothing without measurable, purposeful achievement by leader and led alike. That's PERFORMANCE.

The five Ps are inextricably interwoven. But 5P deployment is above all a test of what guru Daniel Goleman calls 'emotional intelligence' (EI), which is overwhelmingly to do with behaviours involving yourself and others. Here's an EI test. Are you:

- Fully aware of your own abilities, character and limitations?

- In full control of your behaviour – including behaviour towards others?

- Highly motivated towards achieving constructive purposes?

- Aware of, and considerate towards, the feelings and thoughts of others?

- A good mixer, highly effective in groups?

- Able and willing to correct your faults, especially on the five counts above?

Answer the six questions with either ALWAYS, SOMETIMES or NEVER.

If you answer ALWAYS to all six questions, you are almost certainly kidding yourself. These are counsels of perfection, standards from which everybody SOMETIMES departs. But how often is that? Actually, it doesn't matter. One injury to the feelings of others, one failure to keep your eye on the ball of constructive purpose, one loss of control, one failure in self-knowledge – any of these can result in disaster.

Nor can you ignore the fact (widely ignored, just the same) that leadership is a two-way activity. How others respond to your efforts to lead determines your effectiveness. You may have the highest level of EI seen on earth, but that will be useless if you must deal with Six-Never people. Again, their lapses on any of the Goleman Six can vitiate the best intentions of the best leader.

On Mount Elbrus in the Caucasus, almost 1,000 metres higher than Mont Blanc, Rebecca learned the difficulty (which every leader must try to master) of matching your EI to that of others to achieve your purpose. One-man bands, like the notorious crook Robert Maxwell, accomplish this by simply subjugating the led. What you gain in control by dictatorship you lose (maybe doubly, trebly or more) in collaborative action. Maxwell, remember, went ruinously bust.

Worse still, the ablest people will not work for a dominant and irrational tyrant. The richest, greatest, managing tycoon, John D.Rockefeller I, is a role model for leaders in the smallest, youngest business – and all the way upwards, to the largest corporations. He claimed that his immeasurable fortune had been created by his trust in people whom he had given reason to trust him. It's a marvellous formula – one which great leaders often demonstrate.

The following excerpts from a very short speech by Field Marshal Montgomery thus have more than a touch of the Rockefeller recipe. He delivered it to the dejected officers of the battered Eighth Army almost immediately after taking command in 1942. Reading it, you can practically hear the Great Man's voice. It's a small masterpiece, switching from soft to hard and back again. Here is the inspirational opening:

'You do not know me. I do not know you. But we have got to work together – therefore we must understand each other and we must have confidence in each other. I have been here only a few hours. But from what I have seen and heard since I arrived I am prepared to say, here and now, that I have confidence in you. We will then work together as a team'.

There was sterner stuff to follow. Monty noted that:

'... one of the first duties of a leader is to create what I call atmosphere. I do not like the general atmosphere I find here. It is an atmosphere of doubt, of looking back. All that must cease'. He then injected a note of strong purpose. 'I want to impress on everyone that the bad times are over. And it will be done; beyond any possibility of doubt'.

That left no room for what the new General called 'belly-aching', which he had been told was prevalent. He meant by that 'inventing poor reasons for not doing what one has been told to do. All this is to stop at once. If anyone objects to doing what he has been told, then he can get out of it – and at once'. The new leader finished, appropriately and necessarily, on an upbeat:

'[Everybody] must know what is wanted; when they see it come to pass, there will be a surge of confidence throughout. I ask you to give me your confidence; and to have faith that what I have said will come to pass. [Beating Rommel] will be quite easy. We will hit him a crack and finish with him'.

I used the words 'Great Man' above. They certainly apply to Montgomery, although his greatness had yet to be established at the time of his speech. He only achieved heroic status after defeating Rommel at El Alamein. The vast majority of good leaders are by no means Great Men, or anything like. And the Great Man – laden with honours, bowed down before, celebrated, enriched and generally made much of – is not necessarily a great or even a good leader.

Look no further than the horrendous business scandals of the infant twenty-first century in companies mostly dominated by human powerhouses of energy, determination and charisma: like Enron, WorldCom, Tyco, Ahold, Hollinger, Parmalat, Shell and the scam-laden Wall Street investment banks. All these unhappy headliners shared a common factor: either lack of leadership or much too much of the wrong kind.

Identifying wrongness is easier than identifying what constitutes the good in leadership. Creating a rotten, pervasive climate of amoral greed (Enron) is wrong: so is the equally greedy pursuit of headlong, heedless growth by acquisition (WorldCom): so is sustaining unreal growth by tricky accountancy (Ahold), or deliberately inflating vital statistics (Shell): so are alleged thievery (Parmalat) and its close relative, financing a private lifestyle with public company millions (Tyco). As for the Wall Street financiers who aided, abetted and co-authored the frauds, their leadership was kept busy counting its own individual and collective loot.

The obvious negatives do help to establish some of the positives. A good leader, for example, lays down and maintains the basic values of honesty and truthfulness that are vital for good management. But how does the latter differ from good leadership? Everybody knows that good businessmen and women may be bad leaders and poor managers – hence the failures of entrepreneurial businesses that introduce effective management either too late or not at all. But whether a good manager or a good leader can really be bad at business is quite another matter.

I once asked a revered Japanese CEO, Ryuzaburo Kaku of Canon, how it was that he, having spent his whole career in financial functions, had achieved such spectacular success at leading a technology-based company onwards and upwards to world eminence. He was surprised by the question: he wasn't a finance man, he explained politely – he was a businessman. He showed me (as he showed every such visitor, I suspect) an old piece of paper that made his point. As a young executive in finance, he had plotted Canon's profits against its new product introductions. Every time the latter rose, so did profits, after a suitable interval – and *vice versa*.

On achieving power, Kaku promptly followed the logic of his observation, demanding and getting more new products, and reaping the anticipated golden harvest. His master plan was both good business and excellent management. Astute business people know by instinct the key importance of keeping the product or service offer fresh and vibrant. A good manager understands from experience that excellent statistical analysis will tell you where to direct organizational effort in order to obtain the best returns. A good leader ensures that this correct direction is followed.

Ψ

Whether you approach from the business or the managerial or the leadership angle, the next stage is the latter one. Action must follow. Decision without action is no better than indecision: both errors involve expending and wasting much too much valuable energy. In my newspaper days, I worked for two great editors: Sir Gordon Newton of the *Financial Times* and David Astor of the *Observer*. There were immense differences between the two personalities. But the taking, or not taking, of decisions proved critical.

The single-minded, taciturn Newton made his operational decisions at machine-gun speed and with total, unemotional logic. His methods – strong on criticism, weak on praise – didn't earn him the love of his journalists; however grudgingly, though, they gave him their respect. Astor, in contrast, was dearly loved by many and easily outshone Newton in personal charisma. But of Astor it was truly joked that 'The editor's indecision is final': the consequences could be measured, not only in wasted energy, but in lost opportunities – and lost, talented personnel.

Astor was unquestionably a leader. His spirit animated the newspaper and he exerted a real, though strangely diffident personal dominance. But his lack of either managerial intelligence or entrepreneurial push led directly to the newspaper's relative decline and eventual loss of independence. In contrast, Newton's *FT* went rapidly from strength to strength. Leadership qualities can't exist in a vacuum. They are useless unless or until they are applied effectively to real, significant purposes.

The application can't be single-handed, either. The basic definition of leadership involves acting in and through a group, a community. Without followers, there can be no leader. So the role and quality of 'followership' are vital to the nature and success of leadership. It used to be enough for the leader to order and the followers to obey. But not any more. Leaders need understanding of themselves, of their followers, and of the reaction between leader and led in circumstances which are bound to be changeable.

Observe how Montgomery's speech, which led in short order to the historic victories at Alam Halfa and El Alamein, encapsulated all the above truths, and more. I have long used that dynamic address as a text for teaching the Ten Pillars of Leadership:

1   TRUST. The boss (see Rockefeller, also) earns the trust of others by trusting them – and telling them so.

2   TEAMWORK. The leader can only operate together with others, and the more genuine this togetherness, the better the performance will be.

3   CULTURE. Effective collaboration (see 2) depends on the 'atmosphere', which is a prime responsibility of the leader.

4   PURPOSE. The objectives of the enterprise must be sharply defined and pursued with unflagging determination.

5   COMMUNICATION. That purpose must be communicated with total clarity.

6   CONFIDENCE. The self-confidence of the leader or leaders and the confidence of the organization go hand-in-hand.

7   BACK-UP. The confidence will be false unless it is backed by the resources required, and unless actions support the words (Monty duly mentioned that 400 new tanks had just been unloaded at Cairo).

8   PERFORMANCE – the Fifth P of Leadership, and the most important. Full emphasis must be placed on getting done what has to be done, to the standards that must be achieved.

9   HUMANITY. Discipline needs to be tempered with humanity and humour. (Monty told his officers that, whatever their view of his sanity, he wasn't mad; he moved them, too, from horrible quarters to more comfortable, fly-free seaside premises.)

10   COMPETITION. In war, the competitive drive inevitably takes the form of physical, murderous aggression. But the latter shares with its civilian equivalent the 5P requirements, and their intense focus on the task in hand – winning.

The interrelationships of the Ten Pillars, as of the Five Ps, are the essence of real leadership. Both bring equal weight to external and internal considerations, which is crucial. That's why the *Harvard Business Review* warns of 'dissonance between an executive's inside and outside' and insists that 'it's absolutely essential to keep the two aligned'. Alignment is thus one key element in the *HBR*'s special issue on leadership ('Inside the Mind of the Leader', January 2004): another is the aforementioned 'emotional intelligence'. The editors set the latter for discussion by a group of 'business leaders, scholars and other experts', who described 'how to cultivate and manage' EI; while the man who made the concept famous, Daniel Goleman, reported as follows:

'Organizations often implicitly discourage their people from cultivating emotional intelligence. Its chief components – self-awareness, self-regulation, motivation, empathy and social skills – can be learned, but it's not easy.'

Of course, Goleman's five qualities are as valuable in the led as in the leader, who may have none of them. Many highly successful leaders, far from being paragons of EI, are monsters of self-indulgence – they are 'grandiose, actively self-promoting and genuinely narcissistic ... emotionally isolated and highly distrustful ... usually poor listeners ... who lack empathy'. They are also prone to rage. Yet they have 'a great ability to attract and inspire followers'.

The above quotation comes from author Michael Maccoby, whose article originally appeared in the *Review* in 2000. It was reprinted in January 2004 because of the swelling and bursting of the superstar-CEO bubble in the intervening years. As the article points out, the narcissistic personality is ideally suited to thrusting and clawing its way upwards and to maintaining that dominance once arrived at the top. The drive and vision can help to achieve genuine success, but can equally destroy both the company and the leader (see the corporate scams and scandals enumerated earlier).

Yet you're better off with a narcissus, says Maccoby, than you are with the humane 'erotic' personality types. These warm-hearted people 'need too much approval'. As for the third of the main personality types, the 'obsessives' who are driven by efficiency, they make better leaders than erotics, but they act as operational managers. While the obsessives may excel at operations, they prove to be too 'critical and cautious' for entrepreneurial success.

This conflict between the human needs of the group and the inhumane powerhouse qualities of the narcissus is at the root of the leadership paradox. By their very nature, the narcissi tend to win the power and the glory. Should you seek to resist these pocket dictators? Not according to Maccoby, who believes that you just have to grin and bear them. He argues that today's pressures simply increase the need for totalitarian management.

There's a heavy price to pay. Narcissi may well say they want teamwork, when in practice they want only yes-men – and that's the least of their possible defects. Yet more and more large corporations are 'getting into bed' with the narcissists, because they're indispensable in a time when innovation holds the key to growth, profit and survival. So, are grinning and bearing it now part of the standard managerial kit? According to Maccoby, the words mean that you must:

- Always empathize with your boss's feelings, but never expect any empathy in return.

- Give your boss ideas, but always let him or her take the credit for the brainwaves that work.

- Learn how to manage your time efficiently to cope with the narcissist's excessive requests, some of which will make no sense.

Ignore the leader's nonsenses, advises Maccoby cheerfully – just forget them: so will the boss. Frankly, this reads like a toady's charter. You stop short of being a shameless sycophant, but you're supposed to butter up the narcissist's self-image, to take his paranoid views seriously, even to make sure that your free time coincides with the master's.

This subservience to a dominant, untrammelled overlord hardly squares with the ideas proclaimed by the best gurus. They believe (as Rebecca and I do) that the future of management lies with collective, collegiate, bottom-up organizations. These are headed by leaders of leaders – un-bossy bosses who support and facilitate intelligent leadership throughout the organization.

As you would expect, Tom Peters, the leading pundit of the new management, also calls for 'New Leadership ... The Ultimate New Mandate'. For him, one or two ideas are far too few to combat the fact that today leaders and led alike 'don't have a clue' about what's afoot. In a new book, *Re-imagine*! Peters offers no less than 50 leadership ideas, ranging from 'Leaders Say I Don't Know' via 'Leaders Honour Rebels and Hang Out with Freaks' to 'Leaders Know When to Leave' (which notoriously many don't, in business as in politics).

That all sounds fairly revolutionary. But many of the Nifty Fifty would suit a super-boss perfectly – indeed, Peters projects an overall conviction that the Leader is the driving force behind (or rather ahead of) almost everything. His Leaders not only convey the Grand Design, but they attend to the Logistical Details; they Break Down Barriers, Push Their Organizations into the Value-Added Stratosphere, Create New Markets. The image of the business, moreover, is their identity – they are not just the boss, but 'the Brand'.

Disarmingly, Peters concludes that 'all "leadership literature" stinks – including much of the stuff I've written'. That has a simple explanation. The writers all generalize about an activity that has as many facets as there are leaders. The result is conflict and confusion. How can a practising manager/leader make sense out of the Nifty Fifty? How can you reconcile Maccoby's admiration for the indispensable narcissus with Goleman's praise for the emotionally intelligent? The latter are not egotists. They combine a self-deprecating sense of humour with openness to change, expertise in both building and retaining talent, and intelligent persuasion.

The 50th Peters Idea contains a powerful hint at the reconciliation: 'Leaders Do Stuff that Matters'. Leadership hinges round groups and tasks. The leader has to work with the groups, either directly or through delegation, to achieve the overall task and the subordinate tasks that are essential to the whole. The task is to achieve the purpose, and the groups are the combinations of people that are best suited and best organized for the overall and individual purposes. The good leader will concentrate on defining and refining the tasks and optimizing the groups – that's the 'Stuff that Matters'.

What holds all this together is not any one particular leadership or style, certainly not a narcissistic super-ego, but feedback. You need a constant flow of accurate information from the field. That flow will govern the equally constant adaptation of the organization to ensure that the Five Ps of Leadership are working well – Purpose, Plan, Progress and People, all bound together by the essential insistence on Performance.

Sure, the Three Is are enormously important, too – Imagination, Innovation and Inspiration. They may well appear to be the monopoly of a sole leader. There are indeed men and women with powers to imagine, innovate and inspire that far exceed the capabilities of their ablest colleagues. But those powers are not always used to good purposes – merely consider the fanatics and fascists down the ages. And belief in the possession of such powers by the leader of the moment, anyway, is often an irrational and dangerous illusion.

More, who is to know that equal or better visionary powers within the organization are not being suppressed by the dominance of the autocrat? 'The sleep of reason', wrote the artist Goya, 'begets monsters'. Look at those damned companies listed earlier in this chapter, and you'll see the monstrous results that follow when exercise of leadership is left irrationally to the unreasonable leader – and not shared fully by the great community of the led.

SUMMIT 4

- **Don't** employ people **only** on qualifications or experience; **look** closely at how they will perform and contribute in the **future**.

- Step into the shoes of **those you lead** to learn **what they need** in instruction and training.

- **Invest** equal energy **in** developing **staff and yourself**; because leader and led reach the top together - or fail together.

- Have **high expectations** of your people and you will be on the high road to **higher performance**

- **Remember** to say 'thank you'.

- Deploy the **Five Ps of leadership**: Purpose, Plan, Progress, People and Performance.

- Put your **trust** in people who you have given and continue to give good reason to trust you.

- Be a leader of leaders, **supporting and facilitating intelligent leadership** throughout the organization.

- **Concentrate** on the **'Stuff that Matters'** - defining and refining tasks and optimizing the performance of others.

- Remember that the **Three Is** - Imagination, Innovation, and Inspiration – are **vital, but not the sole prerogative** of the leader.

Tapping the Talent 1

CARSTENSZ PYRAMID,
4,884M (16,024FT)

Surrounded by high swampland and dense rainforest, the long limestone fin of Carstensz Pyramid is the highest mountain on the island of New Guinea. It lies in Irian Jaya, the western province of New Guinea, which is today a part of Indonesia – so politically Carstensz Pyramid is in Asia, and its official name is now Mount Jaya. However, in mountaineering circles the former name has stuck. Also, because New Guinea sits on the Australasian continental platform, Carstensz Pyramid is commonly accepted as the highest peak in Australasia. (Its rival is a pimple of a peak called Kosciusko at a ski resort between Melbourne and Sydney.) Due to guerrilla war against Indonesian rule, access to it can be difficult and at times impossible.

Carstensz Pyramid is unique among the Seven Summits in that it is the only one that requires any degree of rock climbing skills – and I am not a rock climber. Faced with a challenge that I was hopelessly ill-equipped to meet, I had three choices. I could give up before I started. Or I could dedicate myself to a rigid training regime to shape myself into some sort of a rock climber, for which frankly there wasn't time if I was to meet my deadline (nor was there the ability). Or else I could accept my inadequacies and ask for help.

Ever pragmatic, it wasn't difficult for me to work out that only the last of the choices would enable me to climb Carstensz Pyramid and in turn the Seven Summits. So, armed with sufficient funding for another expedition member, I approached a friend who is a superb rock climber – a 'crag rat', he's known as – called Graham McMahon and, not surprisingly, considering the opportunity to climb in such an exotic part of the world, he accepted.

So far, so good – except that in inviting Graham I had unwittingly opened a can of worms among the purer thinkers in the climbing fraternity, because Graham wasn't only a friend but also a part-time mountain guide. As on Elbrus, it was a question of mountaineering ethics: 'Wasn't she up to it without a guide?' they asked. 'Can we call this real climbing?' The difference this time, though, was that I took it to heart. On Elbrus I was able to justify inviting Sergei for reasons of safety; and anyway, Elbrus was a high altitude plod – my speciality. But on Carstensz I knew very well that I couldn't make a start on the mountain without Graham. I sympathized with the argument of my critics – although not enough, it must be said, to stop me going with the aid of my helping hand.

In many ways our expedition to Carstensz Pyramid proved to be the most colourful of all the Seven Summits – not so much because of the mountain itself but because of the richness of the journey to it. Carstensz Pyramid is the highest of several 4,000m peaks that make up the Sudirman range in the west of what was formerly Dutch New Guinea, now Irian Jaya. Although the large tropical island itself had been known many years before, the remote western region remained largely undiscovered by Europeans until as late as 1938, when the explorer Richard Archbold flew over the lush Baliem valley and observed numerous huts of the Dani people. And it was not until 1945 that missionaries made contact with these tribespeople, whose numbers were estimated at some 95,000.

Cannibalism, a practice for which the island long had a fearsome reputation, is today a thing of the past, but Irian Jaya is still a difficult, sometimes impossible province in which to travel. Although independent for a short while after the Dutch withdrew from the island in 1963, the people of the newly-named West Papua were quite quickly persuaded by the Indonesian Republic to accept a new government, which, in 1973, formally renamed the province Irian Jaya – Irian, a Biak word meaning 'pretty' (Biak is a small, nearby island), and Jaya meaning 'victory'. For forty years the Organisasi Papu Merdeka, the Free Papua Movement, has waged a nearly constant but so far futile guerrilla war against Indonesian rule.

Graham and I were lucky to get a permit to travel there; another, more troubled year and, as foreigners, we might have been refused. Even so, the permit was severely restricted. We were granted permission to travel from the coastal town of Nabire to the inland village of Ilaga and from there to Carstensz Pyramid, and back again. The first part of the journey was in a Twin Otter, the second by foot – some six days through rainforest and high swampland.

We landed on a small strip of land cleared in the forest just a short walk from Ilaga to discover a village of round, thatched dwellings, sweet potato fields and, as expected, the odd pig. I believe that the villagers were Dani people, originally from the Baliem valley first spotted from the air in 1938. This is a land where men still wear penis gourds and women grass skirts. Little, it seemed, had changed in the passing of the centuries save the occasional constructional addition of well-meaning temporary in-comers: a chapel, a mosque, a police station (of sorts) and a ubiquitous satellite dish.

From the midst of this village of ancient customs juxtaposed to new, Dixon, our interpreter and local guide, invited twenty strong-looking men and women prepared to step in as porters to help carry our mountaineering kit and food to the foot of the mountain. Twenty porters sounds a lot for only two climbers – until one considers the porters' diet. Porters carried sweet potatoes for other porters – great piles of them in loose-woven string bags – and, as the porters ate the potatoes, so they peeled back in pairs to the village. By the time Graham and I found ourselves standing at the foot of a vast slab of corrugated limestone that is Carstensz Pyramid, we were accompanied by just one porter – Alus, an energetic, spirited man – and our interpreter, Dixon.

Ψ

There was no guide book for Carstensz Pyramid. So few people had climbed it that one was hardly justified, and the only information I had on the route was that gleaned from a long distance telephone call with an American who, I had heard, had climbed it.

'There's an odd-shaped rock at the base', he said. 'You'll recognize it when you see it. Take a line up from there to the ridge and then follow the ridge to the summit.'

Sounded straightforward enough. 'There are three notches on the ridge', he added, 'and if there's snow on the mountain, just hang out for a day or two – it'll clear.'

In the grey light of dawn, Graham and I stomped our feet at the base of what we supposed was his odd-shaped rock, and roped up. Graham led and I followed, reaching up and grabbing hold of pin-sharp but satisfyingly large, solid handholds of rock. We had been led to believe the first few pitches were tricky ones.

'It's easy!' I cried (easy to say with a rope securely fastened above my head).

'Hardly a "diff" move on it,' Graham shouted down.

With a lightness in our hearts and our steps we scrambled swiftly up rock and over snow (lots, despite being just south of the equator) and within a couple of hours stood high on the summit ridge, waving and shouting at Alus and Dixon, waving up at us from far below.

'Three hours and we'll crack this,' we agreed, turning our attention to the summit ridge that lay ahead of us. But it was a conservative estimate. Only a few paces along the ridge and we were standing atop a snowy precipice, gazing down into the first of our American friend's notches. It was about twenty metres deep with a steep rock wall both into it and out of it the other side.

'It's impossible,' I said.

But Graham stood calm. 'Let's get down into it and have a look,' he suggested matter-of-factly. He fixed an anchor for the rope and instructed me to abseil down into the notch, which I did, the full length of the rope, until, with a small fluttering of the heart, my feet touched the rock beneath me.

Graham followed me down and the two of us stood on a precariously tiny platform of rock, the mountain falling away to our left and right, looking up at the rock face straight in front of us. I didn't say a word. This was Graham's territory, way beyond anything I could imagine doing myself. I watched him as he watched the rock, examining its cracks and crevasses, its tiniest knobbles and dents, reading it for its best line of ascent. And then I watched him turn in one sweeping movement and pull down the abseil rope from the rock face we had just descended. We were committed now. Our route was up the face in front of us, and on. We roped up and Graham reached for the first hold on the face ahead. A handhold, a foothold, another handhold – gracefully he manoeuvred his way up the face like a gymnast, which he is – and I watched, mesmerized.

He was at the top. I waited while he secured an anchor, then 'Climb when you're ready!' he cried, and I made my way up the face – once again with the comfort of a rope above my head.

There were, as the American rightly informed us, three notches on the ridge, one with an overhang that had me spiralling a dizzy 360° on the abseil rope, empty space below my feet and all around me. But in each one Graham read the rock like a book and climbed up onto the ridge the other side with grace and style. And I followed, with total confidence in Graham's ability, doubting nothing.

Nonetheless, it took a good deal longer to progress along the ridge than we'd estimated at the start. There was a lot of snow. 'It'll melt,' the American had said, but not for several days. It was up to our knees and slushy, and our feet, in leather boots, were soaked; our hands cold. Four hours passed, maybe five; then, 'We'll give it an hour,' Graham said, all voice of reason, 'and I think we should maybe turn back.'

It took a moment for me to register what he'd said. Turn back? No way! Time was racing but we had bivouac bags and a stove; we would sleep where we stood if it came to it. I suddenly felt called upon to inject a little urgency into our venture: 'Here, an almond slice,' I said, 'now let's get going.'

In the event we didn't go for an hour; we hardly went another fifteen minutes. A couple of hundred metres of easy ground and we stood, pleased as punch, on the summit. We were benighted on the way down and it took us an age to get to our camp at the foot of the mountain, but we'd climbed it – that was important.

REFLECTIONS

I once heard it said at a lecture by the philosopher Alain de Botton: if you are suffering anxiety about your relatively impoverished position in society, a sure remedy is to delete all your most successful friends from your Christmas card list. You'll feel a lot better!

A gentle chuckle rippled through the audience, for I don't suppose there was one of us who didn't in some way relate to this sorry tale, revealing as it did the sensitivity of a part of our inner being – namely the ego.

He went on to make the point that when comparing ourselves and our position with others in society we rarely feel anxious when that comparison is with someone whose status and wealth is unimaginable, like, say, the Queen. That would be ludicrous, because for most of us no amount of effort could result in attaining such a position.

We might, however, feel a twinge of anxiety if we were to attend a reunion of old school friends, say, to discover that these old muckers of ours had somehow acquired country houses, swimming pools and smart husbands and wives. Why? Because their obvious success highlights our own inadequacies, it shines a spotlight on what might have been different if only we had been smarter, more talented or simply harder working. As someone once said (can't remember who; must have been someone ambitious): 'on hearing of a friend's success, a small part of me dies'.

Not everybody will compare themselves with others in such status-conscious terms, of course, or indeed want to. But it does lead me onto the subject of the ego which was very definitely at play when I invited along Graham to help me climb Carstensz Pyramid, and which can also be at play in the workplace.

In inviting along Graham, my ego wasn't so much bruised by his obvious, shining talent as a rock climber (like aspiring to the riches of the Queen, that would have been ridiculous!), but by the criticism of others that in some way I wasn't up to the job, that the venture I was embarking on wasn't what might be called 'real climbing'.

I knew then, as I know now, that in this regard I failed. I am not a competent rock climber and I'm never going to be. But as some consolation I think I can say that together we made a successful team – and that is as relevant in our working lives as it is in the mountain.

The most important lesson that I learned on Carstensz Pyramid was one of humility. I learned that by recognizing my limitations and, importantly, declaring them to another member of the team who was in a position to help – namely, Graham – I wasn't in any sense weakening the overall strength of the team but conversely I was strengthening it by giving Graham a true sense of self-worth (I *needed* him) and a responsibility to give it his best. Declaring my vulnerability served only to strengthen the bond, like a good friendship or marriage

To conclude, we don't build successful teams by striking off the best talent from our Christmas card list. Quite the opposite; we build strong, effective working teams by inviting on board the brightest, most highly skilled, most talented and motivated individuals we can find. And if this only serves to highlight our own inadequacies, then we quietly take ourselves off into a corner and have a little chat with ourselves. We remind ourselves that we, too, have an important role to play, and that is to steer the collective genius of the team to meet its set objectives.

It's a win/win situation. By surrounding oneself with the best people, the team as a whole is strengthened, and, in the resultant creation of a stimulating environment, the individual is inspired to improve performance as well. To fall back on another sporting analogy, one's game of tennis is only improved by playing with people better than oneself.

Tapping the Talent 2

Bad managers are frightened of employing good people with brains and skills that surpass their own. Good managers are delighted. Surround yourself with shining talent and you lighten your own load, enhance the collective power of the team, and turn deficiencies into assets. That's why picking superior talent is a priceless skill.

Turn to any corporate triumph, and exceptional talents are always at the root of the organization's achievements. Superior hiring and development, for example, basically gave Marks & Spencer, in its palmy post-war years, its golden reputation (now sadly tarnished) as a world-class management machine; even the best of the best. Talented orchestration, too, explains much of Microsoft's unbeatable late-century ascendancy, as the hugely brainy Bill Gates relentlessly sought others with intellectual 'bandwidth'.

Tapping the talent, not least at the corporate summit, powered the unexampled twenty years of wealth creation recorded by General Electric under Jack Welch. Spotted early on, and rising fast, Welch became CEO aged 45, nominated by an incumbent, Reginald Jones, who deliberately picked somebody very different from himself: a man who, to quote a *Fortune* writer, had a 'tendency to rattle cages and shake things up ... exactly what Jones wanted'.

It was exactly what Welch delivered, earning the nickname 'Neutron Jack' from the bomb that kills people but leaves buildings intact. After this ruthless managerial pruning, Welch concentrated on constructive strategies that saw an immense rise in 'shareholder value'. But from the start of his second decade, like Jones before him, Welch turned to the succession, saying in 1991: 'From now on, choosing my successor is the most important decision I'll make. It occupies a considerable amount of thought every day'.

What else would you expect? The same care, concentration and thought that elevated Jeffrey Immelt to succeed Welch should surely apply, not just at the peak, but the whole way down the mountain. The boast that 'people are our most important asset' may conceal a whole load of self-deception, but it also enshrines powerful truth – though not the whole truth. That is more cogently expressed by declaring that 'people are our most important *product*'; because the life and death of organizations revolve around the intricate, interlocking processes of winning talent and exploiting its full powers over many and long careers.

Year by year, the able people and the admirable institution should advance in step, reinforced by the new top talents acquired and enhanced over time. The multi-faceted task of producing prize people runs the gamut of ten processes – how people are:

1 *Recruited*. Did you form a clear picture of who you wanted and what for?

2 *Monitored*. If you'd known then what you know now, would you still have appointed/promoted this person? If not, what went wrong?

3 *Trained*. Starting with induction, do you ensure that people always get all the information and skills necessary to do a superb job?

4 *Developed*. Do you accept your full share of the responsibility for helping people to build successful careers?

5 *Promoted*. Do you advance them as rapidly as possible so that they can fully use, and enlarge, their experience and expertise?

6 *Recognized*. Do you and the company have ways of making people feel good about what they've achieved and how they are regarded?

7 *Rewarded*. Are people given exceptional rewards for exceptional performance – including exceptional contributions to the team?

8 *Organized*. Is the management system set up and constantly revised to ensure that it facilitates, and doesn't impede, initiative and achievement?

9 *Motivated*. Do you and the company use every possible means of encouraging self-motivation?

10   *Mobilized.* Are people and teams pointed in the right direction and given motivating tasks at the right time?

This is an intimidating, but indispensable catechism. Its lessons can't be dodged. Welch's progress and his promotion of others rub them in at every point. As example, here are his criteria for his own succession: he was looking for somebody who had:

- Incredible energy

- Ability to excite others

- Ability to define a vision

- Finds change fun and not paralyzing

- Feels comfortable in Delhi or Denver

- Can talk to all kinds of people.

That doesn't sound as if Welch, unlike Jones, was searching for a replacement markedly different from himself. As a rule, powerful bosses should never appoint their own successors – they will subconsciously name an inferior who will not surpass them. Maybe Immelt will prove an exception, like Welch himself. But make a mistake in any of these ten processes, which apply at all levels of the firm, and all the previous expenditure of energy (on both sides of the employment relationship) is liable to run to waste.

Ψ

Rebecca wasn't exactly an employer on the Seven Summits, but her conquest was in many respects a model of manpower management by womanpower. For instance, it isn't feasible, even with exemplary policies, to rely solely on internal promotion. Sometimes tapping outside talent isn't a luxury, but an essential. Rebecca had to confront this truth when about to tackle Carstensz Pyramid in Indonesia, the highest peak in Australasia: height wasn't her problem – but rock-climbing was required, and Rebecca (as she confesses in the previous chapter) was no rock climber.

The convincing reason for hiring management consultants is to buy in irreplaceable missing skills. Rebecca duly hired a rock-climbing ace (or 'crag rat') to take her to the peak. Such acts of appointment aren't abdication. Apart from the sheer common sense of seeking expert help, making effective use of people who outperform you is no mean skill – and vital in a business world where complexities (and thus needs for expertise) are expanding exponentially.

The basic task in managing talent, though, lies not in recruiting superb outsiders, but in finding, nurturing and deploying superior talent inside the organization. The telltale sign of turn-of-century decline at M&S was its seeming inability to bring forward brilliant top leadership from its own ranks. The fabled family succession from Simon Marks to his brother-in-law and intimate partner, Israel Sieff, and from Israel to his son Marcus, had worked so smoothly that it disguised shortcomings bubbling away below the dynasts.

In hindsight, a disconcerting number of high-fliers, younger men who had flown near the summit, had left, rather than bid for the final eminence. The family genius departed with the family, but the father-knows-best tradition continued into a period in which different, radical and original talents were required at the summit – and below.

In the longer term, the most valuable talent in any organization is not whoever occupies the top slot, draws the top reward and makes all the top decisions. That high-and-mighty personage will be gone and maybe dead when today's younger talents should be commanding the future (now the present) that they have largely shaped. Their ability and their contributions should be decisive well before they take over formal authority.

As Jack Welch knew and demonstrated at GE, a chief executive cannot pass the time more usefully than in spotting, developing and exploiting his talent bank. But the psychological difficulty is clear. The full results of this youthful activity, for good or ill, will not appear in the current CEO's executive lifetime. The four-colour cover of *Business Week* or *Fortune* (or both) will be only too apparent in the here and now, along with laudatory stories hymning the hero's exploits.

'Stories' is *le mot juste*. The journalist will do an ace job of expert reporting. But the article, however long, is a snapshot, not an X-ray. By its very nature, a story placing the CEO at stage centre gets the human dimension wrong. A most perceptive guru, the sharp-eyed (and tongued) Henry Mintzberg, got it pithily right, remarking on some fulsome praise of the achievements at IBM of one Lou Gerstner, 'all by himself?'

Just as Hillary and Tenzing required many helping hands and legs to make that first, epochal ascent of Everest, so the performance of the 'top' talent ('top' in the hierarchical sense) is the sum of all the talents available to the firm. The one talent that can be dispensed with is unfortunately dominant (literally so): despotism. Business history is littered with fallen idol corporations that were run, and often created, by dominant supremos, lords of the universe, who allowed no rivals near the throne.

While the force is with them, despots can succeed brilliantly; too often, the once all-conquering drive turns inwards, and an arrogant, obsolescent leader makes bad and badly executed decisions, which are all the worse for lack of opposition. This type of personality is also expert at appointing heirs apparent, often imported from another company, and then assassinating the potential upstart.

Some despots have no talent other than that of domineering. Even that helps in getting things done, or *Making It Happen* (the title of the admirable book on essential management by Sir John Harvey-Jones). Equally valuable is the talent for seeing what 'It' should be - spotting and grasping the vision. The mountaineer has the visionary objective provided by nature. But John Hunt, when leading the first successful ascent of Everest, still needed strength of personal vision and powers of organizing the talents of others.

Without these powers, Hunt's expedition would certainly have failed; Tenzing and Hillary would never have raised their flag. Despots, however, are seldom smart at selecting and developing the best supporting talent - especially for tasks, such as establishing orderly and effective management processes, for which they have little aptitude or enthusiasm themselves. The need for professional management becomes obvious, and so is the solution - to import seasoned talent to supplement and preferably replace one-person eccentricity (and egocentricity) with proper systems and a true management team.

Ψ

So much for the ideal. What about reality? The deeply embarrassing, public and prolonged row over the succession at M&S culminated in one unsuccessful appointment after another, both internal and external. No doubt, the store chain had 'proper systems and a strong management team', but both were misfiring in marketplace and boardroom alike. Succession is the ultimate test of top management, and its failure, instead of being common, should be unthinkable.

In 1973, Welch's GE mentor noted approvingly, in a rave review of his protégé, 'Another key result. Clearly developed a runner-up for his job in event of promotion'. Every manager needs to be responsible for ensuring that fully equipped talents are waiting in the wings as replacements. Actually, 'waiting in the wings' is a misleading metaphor. The candidates should be fully occupied in active work that constantly tests and demonstrates their skills, prepares them for the next climb and brings them into close contact with whoever appoints them.

In almost all cases, 'whoever' means the Old Guard. It appoints the New; but is that the best and only way? Ricardo Semler, owner of Semco, a middling-sized Brazilian engineering company, is world-famous for eccentric but effective policies. And his quirks include having people vote on whether to accept those nominated as their bosses (who must present their case before a staff meeting).

The idea of team members having a say in who joins them and, above all, who acts as their leader makes critical sense when approaching a dangerous mountain. It's no less sensible in organizations. Semler goes further by also giving workers the right to judge their leader's performance. A carefully constructed questionnaire is scored: falling below a given percentage may well be fatal to the unlucky leader, since it calls into question his or her ability to lead.

Management with the consent of the managed is as fundamental as government with the consent of the governed. Consent illumines the Five Critical Behaviours embedded in these questions. Do you (or does your boss):

1   Help people to create ACHIEVEMENT (reaching or exceeding their strategic objectives)?

2   Give them full RECOGNITION for doing so?

3   Sustain JOB INTEREST by encouraging positive satisfaction?

4   Give real, personal RESPONSIBILITY?

5   Reflect its successful exercise with ADVANCEMENT?

Observe that the active role here is not reserved for the employee: the manager has a leading part at every stage. It follows that the manager shares both the success and the failure of the managed. You appoint the best candidates on objective criteria and leave them free to run their responsibilities – unless poor results reveal their incompetence. But that incompetence also reflects on your own. Either you hired the wrong person or you handled the right person wrongly. Or perhaps the mistake lay not in the hiring, but the firing.

The employee deserves a goodly quantity of benefit of the doubt. It's generally foolish (and cruel) to expel people for one mistake. Dismissal should follow only when the errors betray an underlying pattern of failure, coupled with inability or reluctance to learn its lessons. You're not a referee giving a red card for a single bad transgression. Like success, failure requires analysis and understanding. In particular, what part did the boss play in creating the conditions for failure?

• Did the person get the required autonomy?

• Was there satisfactory back-up in terms of resources – financial, technological, human, etc?

- Were the control mechanisms sensitive and supportive?

- Was the appointee encouraged to follow the same principles in dealing with his or her own subordinates?

- Was enough time allowed for the person to show their capabilities?

These enabling provisions are the key to managing exciting talent – a need that is not confined to businesses with especially obvious creative requirements, like the arts, entertainment, media, advertising and high-tech. The demands of the genius art director or chip designer for empowerment and recognition exist strongly in people with much less exciting roles. That doesn't mean all people. Some employees do seem entirely devoid of ambition, know-how, enthusiasm and other drivers.

These malcontents and misfits, however, are not the only types you need to consider. There's a simple matrix that compels objective analysis of the entire crew. The matrix only has two dimensions. Is the person able to do the job (CAN DO) or unable (CAN'T DO)? Are they willing to work (WILL DO) or unwilling (WON'T DO)? The malcontent misfit is obviously a CAN'T DO, WON'T DO, and there's little to be done save curse yourself for a bad hiring decision and end the agony (which is probably mutual) as quickly and fairly as possible.

In the opposite square of the matrix there's equally small room for uncertainty. The CAN DO, WILL DO type is the ideal employee or ally. Such people require – and deserve – the full treatment in the Five Critical Behaviours listed above. That leaves the two problem categories: CAN'T DO, WILL DO and CAN DO, WON'T DO. The first is the easiest to handle, provided the basic human material is present. Providing the necessary knowledge, know-how and practice will then create another marvellous CAN DO, WILL DO – and few experiences in management are more satisfying and rewarding, for both parties.

CAN DO, WON'T DO seldom gives a result that either satisfies or rewards. The saying goes that there are no bad soldiers, only bad officers. Few who have served in the Army will agree. There may well be cases where a naturally lazy, recalcitrant (or 'Bolshie') worker has been transformed into a CAN DO, WILL DO. But place your bets elsewhere – and reflect on another cliché; that leopards seldom change their spots.

But, to repeat, there are bad officers – and how: the poor motivation and performance may indeed result from miserable management. For all its simplicity, the CAN/WILL matrix has to be used with great care and sensitivity. Other time-worn metaphors also apply. Is the person a square peg in a round hole? Are you giving a dog a bad name? In the first instance, moving them to the right job will work speedy miracles. In the second, the human dog will live down to your expectations – which may be wholly unjustified.

Some five-star American companies take dog-naming all too seriously. Jack Welch's GE (like Bill Gates's Microsoft and Andy Grove's Intel) ran on a stern grading system. A manager who delivered on performance commitments and shared the company's people-based values made Welch's Type I. Not meeting the commitments or sharing the values put the manager in Type II. Missing the commitments, but sharing the values, is Type III. Finally, Type IV delivers the commitments, but doesn't share the values.

Welch dealt with this quartet via the three Rs – REWARD, REMOVAL, REPETITION. Type I got rewarded with progress and promotion. Type II was summarily removed. Type III got a second chance (repetition), preferably somewhere else in the company. As for the valuable but value-less Type IVs, unless they changed their ways (very hard for such types), they suffered the same summary fate as the useless Type IIs.

The GE approach bears a resemblance to the CAN/WILL matrix, but that is superficial. The matrix seeks to be factual on both CAN and WILL; the typecasting at GE depends on value judgements (so to speak) about the observance of values. Some of these are hard to pin down. How do you prove 'a passion for excellence and hatred of bureaucracy'? Or measure 'the self-confidence to involve everyone and behave in a boundaryless manner?'

The dog-naming systems are reminiscent of the slam-bang technique used by high-pressure sales managements. Here, reps are ranked monthly by their sales, and the bottom seller gets dropped off the ladder. The cruel idiocy of the procedure was mercilessly exposed by the late, masterly guru W. Edwards Deming. He put the onus overwhelmingly on management. Managers, he declared, created the system, which workers were powerless to change, but which determined 85% of their output.

Deming pointed out that, even within a bunch of Type I, CAN DO/WILL DO superstars, somebody has to come bottom of any ranking. This result is nothing but random, and meaningless in the context of the performance of the entire team. Raising that performance as a whole is therefore the logical, scientific policy. Hire-and-fire regimes are a bad substitute for genuine managing. That involves judging people on their merits, and providing help if those qualities, for whatever reason, are not achieving meritorious performance.

Appraisal systems are designed to monitor performance, and maintain its standards on a continuous basis; just as naming targets, as in the once popular Management by Objectives, is supposed to semi-automatically lead to their achievement. But managers dislike conducting appraisal interviews, and most subordinates are no more enthusiastic about being appraised. As for objectives, the Blair government in Britain has provided numerous grisly examples of their distorting effect as people concentrate on what's targeted at the expense of what's important.

You are dealing with human beings, after all, and they are complex, sensitive pieces of machinery. In post-war years, there's been a welcome, fairly continuous and reasonably widespread movement away from rigid systems backed by the authoritarian use of the carrot and the stick. This is the seminal shift from Order and Obey (or Command and Control) to Advise and Consent. The latter phrase derives from the constitutional relationship between the US President and the Senate, and egalitarian democracy is at the heart of twenty-first century people management.

Ψ

You can't climb mountains safely and successfully without the full participation of your equals. The familiar acronym for people management is relevant in the Himalayas too – ARM, for Attract, Retain and Motivate – but there are deep differences. You want to attract the best climbers available, but they are highly self-motivated and unlikely to desert the climb without compelling reason. Yet for all the differences, the mountains offer a most valuable lesson on the ground. Motivation by others is not what you're after: self-motivation has to be the aim.

It goes hand-in-hand with self-management. People with talent thrive on freedom and are stultified by restraint. Freedom has to be combined with discipline, but, again, self-discipline is much more effective than discipline imposed and operated from above. The progressive thesis has always been that people work better when they are treated with respect; trusted to carry out tasks they enjoy; and given an environment of shared responsibility and positive friendship between colleagues who like each other.

But the role of management in developing the relationship between talent and the organization is pivotal. Talented people need to be treated as partners, not dependants. The ideal is to have the talent do what you (and they) want, not what you order. Ambitious employers of talent are deeply interested in the output, not in how that output is achieved. And if, to get the desired outcome, they have to allow mavericks and zanies to behave in maverick and zany ways, that's the world as it is. Get it on your side – and your mountainside.

SUMMIT 5

- **Recognize**, declare and offset **your own limitations** when recruiting and deploying people who are genuine 'partners'.

- Show the strength of your own ego by freely acknowledging the **superior talents of others**.

- Always **listen** to critics, but accept or **act** on criticism only when you know it to be **right**.

- **Steer** the collective genius of the **talents** you recruit **towards** meeting the team's **set objectives**.

- **Dream** the dream, **share** it with everybody and use it to **drive** them and the enterprise **upwards**.

- Master and **apply** consistently all **ten processes** involved in surrounding yourself with **outstanding talent**.

- Rely on **expert help**, making effective use of people, internal and external, who can fill the gaps.

- **Give less creative** people the **same** stimulus, independence and encouragement that **creatives** demand.

- Help to **create achievement**, give it **full recognition**, sustain **job interest**, give real **responsibility** – and **reward** success with advancement.

- Aim to **work** only with CAN DO, WILL DO colleagues who combine excellent **abilities** with high and constant **self-motivation**.

Thinking Positively 1

ACONCAGUA, 6,960M (22,834FT)

Aconcagua is the highest mountain in the western and southern hemispheres – the second highest of the Seven Summits. Impressive rather than beautiful, it lies to the east of the main Andean chain, just inside Argentina's border with Chile, visible from the Pacific coast, 100 miles away. Shaped like a great wedge, it is known as the 'stone sentinel' because its summit and ridges are largely windswept free of snow, although large glaciers fill the valleys on the northern and eastern flanks. Relatively straightforward to climb, it nonetheless has one of the world's highest death tolls because of its elevation and severe weather.

The wind blew and by God it was cold. I made the mistake of taking off my gloves – for twenty seconds, no more. The warmth drained from my fingers like water from a jug, and I felt a panic rising inside me. I must act, now! Stumbling across the rocks I threw myself bodily into the tent where my climbing companion, John, mercifully cupped my stiffened hands in his. Then, prising open my fingers, he gazed, in horror, at my palms. They were dappled in ugly patches of frost-nip.

I wondered in that moment if we would make it.

We were on Aconcagua, a monster of a peak in the Andean range, dull to the eye, like a giant slag heap, and savagely inhospitable – and, importantly from my point of view, the highest peak in South America. This was the crux of the Seven Summits, the mountain my competition had already climbed and I had to attempt in October, out of season, when hurricane-force winds and frighteningly low temperatures kept more prudent climbers at bay.

More than anything, climbing Aconcagua was an exercise in positive thinking. I spoke to a dozen people at the planning stage who told me that to climb it in October was inadvisable; and then I spoke to one – a Chilean climber, in Santiago – who gave me hope. 'If you're lucky,' he said, 'and you've got time, there might be a short lull in the weather and you might, just, make it to the summit.'

We had to give it a go. The timing wasn't ideal, but then, the time one's called upon to act in life is often far from the most convenient. It would be a battle. No doubt about that. But if we have set our hearts on achieving something we must accept that for a limited period of time, at least, we can forget the notion of relaxation and play. Climbing Aconcagua would be a dedicated, focused effort, calling upon all my resolve. I couldn't make the mountain smaller, or the weather more clement; but I could focus more intently on my objective to climb the Seven Summits, and I could, at the planning stage, take steps to leave as little as possible to chance.

I carried the lesson of preparation and contingency planning from John's leadership on Denali. I knew that we must have the warmest boots and clothing money could buy and plentiful supplies of fuel and food – easy things to organize with a little forethought. We must also give ourselves as much time as was possible. To set off too early at the start would be to invite even more ferocious weather upon ourselves, and the closing deadline was fixed by the flight time scheduled from Punta Arenas to Antarctica, for me to climb the last of the Seven Summits. But there was still room for a little manoeuvring: I could book a seat on my connecting flight from Santiago to Punta Arenas on not just one flight but two – the first leaving a comfortable margin to catch the Antarctic flight and the second a tight, but still feasible one.

Importantly, I must also ensure that we had not two or three climbers on the team, but four, so that should one fall sick, or succumb to the altitude (of which there was a fair chance at 6,960m), then we could break into two teams of two and not leave anybody on their own.

The team was a strong one. There was John, who had led our expedition on Everest, Dave Halton, a climber on that same team, and a new character in the mix – Martin Barnicott (Barny, we called him) – who had floated up Everest the year before.

And as luck would have it, the last contingency plan was called upon early, even before we had reached the high camp on the mountain. Barny, who had met no apparent problems at extreme altitude on Everest, started to cough up blood – and Dave Halton, in an act of extreme concern and generosity, gave up his own bid for the summit to accompany him down.

That might have left only John and me with a chance to make it to the summit – except that there were two other climbers foolhardy enough to be on the mountain at the time – both British, as it happened, and both, like me, intent on climbing Aconcagua and then heading south to climb Vinson in Antarctica. The two of them were ensconced in a tent at some 5,951m – our high camp – next to us.

It was at the high camp that I made the mistake of removing my gloves – only for a matter of seconds – and watched the blood drain from my hands. It was frighteningly cold. For two days we were tent-bound, unable to move. Both afternoons there was a white-out – we couldn't see our hands in front of our faces – and in the evenings lenticular cloud streaked the sky. I hardly dared step out of the tent for fear of being plucked into the air like a dead twig or leaf, and dumped on the ground. Yet inside the tent the mood was gloomy – if bad weather forced us to wait very much longer, I would miss my flights to Antarctica.

On the last day that we could possibly climb to the summit and still hope to catch the first of my two connecting flights from Santiago to Punta Arenas, we decided that we would give it a go. Our British neighbours, too, made the same decision.

Early in the morning, as John and I went through the usual ritual of preparation for a climb, we watched as the two climbers left the camp ahead of us and slowly made their way up the mountain – and then, after climbing only a couple of hundred metres, turn around. In minutes they were back at the camp. 'It's too cold,' they said, struck their tent, and left.

'Too cold,' I repeated under my breath. If it was too cold for these two men who between them had clocked up winter ascents of some major peaks and walked to both north and south poles, then ... possibly! ... it was too cold for me.

But not so, thought John. It might be too cold for them, he said, but that didn't mean to say that it was too cold for him. I couldn't help but smile, marvelling at both his arrogance, and his confidence.

Nonetheless, we didn't go anywhere that day. Their verdict rather put us off. But the next day – the very last day that we could possibly afford to climb if I was to catch the second (and last) of my connecting flights to Punta Arenas – we gave it a shot.

Ψ

The going was relatively straightforward at first. It was windy, but I had grown acclimatized to this: only twice was I physically knocked off my feet.

'I think we can do this', I said, suddenly overcome with a burst of optimism.

'Just worried about the wind on the ridge', retorted John. Directly above us lay a snowy crest and if, as we feared, we might have to inch our way along it, we were finished. It would be suicidal in these winds. My mood took a momentary dive as we climbed towards it, but within minutes John, ahead of me, was standing on top of the crest, beaming down at me.

I joined him and all became clear. The route to the summit didn't lie along the length of the crest, as we'd feared, but over the top of it, into a broad sweeping col the other side.

'Wind's strong, though', said John, ever the master of understatement. I could barely stand up.

'Hey, it's your Seven Summits, not mine', he yelled. The wind whipped away his words. 'We can go on, or turn back', he said, 'I've really enjoyed the battle today but I'm happy to turn back.'

John was always good in a scrap. 'It's your decision', he said.

Dear Lord, I hate this. I looked across the col. The path, though gently angled, seemed to go on for ever. But did I want to come back to this mountain if we failed?

No, never.

And did I want to go on and climb Vinson and the Seven Summits?

Yes, of course I did.

Strangely, as we battled our way along the path, we grew acclimatized to the haunting screams of the wind. To be buffeted and bashed became almost the norm; and then, as the clouds closed in, as they had the afternoon before, and the afternoon before that, the wind dropped a little. Miraculously we found ourselves standing above the storm, looking down upon it swelling in the valley below us.

If we thought our troubles were over, though, we only had to look up, towards the summit, to be proved wrong. The penultimate leg of Aconcagua is the Canalete, a steep attic stairway of loose, rolling scree leading to the final ridge. And we were high now – over 6,500m. It was back to step counting: one, two, three, and I'd slip back two, all the while nausea rising in voluminous waves from my stomach.

I felt rotten to the core and climbed at an infinitesimally slow pace. John must have been concerned. Only 100m or so from what, on repeated, hopeful examination I imagined to be the summit, he signalled to me that perhaps I might want to go down.

Was he crazy?

It took me the best part of an hour to stumble the last 100m, but, finally, I lifted my exhausted body onto the summit plateau and there was John, holding a shining metal cross that shouted in all its heavenly symbolism; we've done it! This was the crux of the Seven Summits, and we'd done it! The view from the summit took my breath away. Just inches from where we stood, the snow-fluted South Face of the mountain fell away as a near-vertical precipice, plummeting some 3,000m to its base. This was the steep edge of the Aconcaguan wedge, and I registered it in my mind's eye for something less than a second – and then, the altitude defeating me, I was violently sick.

We didn't hang around for long. The sun hung low in the sky and we had very few daylight hours to return to our camp. Dusk fell and still we were descending. Then darkness fell. As we lost altitude I felt stronger with every step; my nausea dissipated as if I were on a boat just sailed into harbour.

But, stupidly, we couldn't find our camp. Were we above it still? Or had we dropped below it? In the pitch darkness we lost all sense of orientation and simply couldn't work it out, although our suspicion was that we had climbed too low. In the uncertainty of the camp's position, neither of us could face climbing back up the mountain on the chance that we'd trip over the guy ropes. And to keep climbing, down, down, down to the base camp would be suicidal; precipices loomed left and right. So we stopped where we were. Like a pair of penguins we huddled together for warmth, against a rock as some sort of protection from the wind – and together sat it out through the night. It was desperately cold, but no temperature could have been too bitter or wind too ferocious for me that night. My spirits soared. We had climbed Aconcagua, the mountain that had been enshrouded with uncertainty from the start, and ahead of us was a clear run.

REFLECTIONS

It was Aconcagua that taught me just how powerful is the concept of positive thinking, particularly when it reinforces an inherent want. ' You might, just, make it to the summit,' said my Chilean friend. From which I concluded, it's not impossible then? So it must be possible. I so badly wanted to climb it that I flatly refused to take on board the negative, and hung onto those few positive words with all my heart.

Every one of us on the team had to hold onto this positive attitude when, walking to the mountain, we met a small band of climbers walking the other way, their heads hung low and their hands frostbitten and bandaged. Hardly an auspicious start! But, we thought, the weather will be kinder to us. And when the weather wasn't kinder to us ... well, I nearly faltered, and would have done had it not been for John.

The day our British neighbours at the high camp headed down with the parting words, 'It's too cold', I would have packed my bags and parted, too. Except that I was fortunate enough to be in the company of John who held fast. It might be too cold for them, he said, but that didn't mean to say that it was too cold for him.

The two British climbers are cold-climate men; but then so, too, is John. He had served in the Mountain and Arctic Warfare Cadre of the Royal Marines and scaled a number of Himalayan peaks. But the lesson I learned from Aconcagua was that to compare only the physical toughness of these men was missing the point. Just as important – more important, indeed – was their attitude. Did our neighbours want to climb Aconcagua as badly as John? And as me? And were they adequately prepared?

The answer to the first question is 'unlikely'; their focus was on Antarctica, not Aconcagua – they had just thought it a fun idea to stop over in Santiago and climb Aconcagua while in that part of the world, so to speak. And were they prepared? Simply put, no. They left a set of very useful warm clothes in Santiago. On this one occasion, these two extremely tough, competent climbers – well able to climb Aconcagua in the conditions we experienced that day – had underestimated the scale of the challenge they had set themselves.

This has instilled in me a way of thinking that I use in my everyday and working life. Whenever people say to me that something is too difficult, even impossible, I think, 'for you maybe, but not necessarily for me'. It might sound arrogant (as I thought John) but the fact is that whether something is possible or impossible depends not only on skill and experience but on circumstance, approach, planning and also a positive attitude and desire to achieve. There's a phrase for this as old as the hills: where there's a will there's a way.

Lastly our experience in such extreme conditions on Aconcagua reinforced the importance of a mutual trust among players in a team. Crucially John and I had clocked up some time together in the hills and understood one another's strengths and weaknesses. We understood the scale of the challenge and the responsibility to watch out for one another along the way. To climb in such dire conditions was a decision we took together, it wasn't one that was decided for us by anybody else. And this, I believe, was the only responsible way we could have undertaken such a challenge – a lesson that was to be extremely relevant for the mountain ahead.

Thinking Positively 2

The legendary American football coach, Knut Rockne of Notre Dame, once averred that 'Winning isn't the most important thing in life. It's the only thing'. This very positive thought is so pithy and powerful that it's been attributed to other, more recent sporting figures. Of course, you don't and can't always win. But that's never a reason for not trying. To secure her funding, Rebecca was determined to complete the Seven Summits before another Brit, Dr Ginette Harrison. Without that determination, Rebecca would never have risked climbing Aconcagua in October's hazardous weather.

This was definitely 'a stretching target'. Too often managers dogmatically set such targets for subordinates. The winning trick, though, is to let the managed form the positive expectations that lead to triumph. It must be *their* decision, not one forced upon them by others. Ask a team if they can launch a new car from scratch in 14 months, as with the LandRover Discovery, leave the willing soldiers to fill in and fulfil the plan, and the results may stagger everybody – including the competition.

As Rebecca found on Aconcagua, a very high 6,960m (22,834 ft), cold and windy peak, the highest in South America, it's of absolute importance, in an extreme situation, for everybody to understand the urgency and the risks. Mastering tough competition, especially against the odds, is undoubtedly extreme. Winning the war demands:

- Positive thinking at all times.

- Building contingency plans to minimize the risk of failure.

- Keeping the vision, fuelled by desire, clearly in mind.

- Keeping your nerve, especially when others are losing theirs.

Bill Gates kept his nerve and vision intact when (thanks to his own gross misjudgement) Netscape and its web browser threatened to drain Microsoft's lifeblood. In this crisis, created by a surprising failure to recognize the unfolding immensity of the Internet, Gates won stern internal and external battles to emerge with the company more powerful, more dominant than ever. That's positive thinking to the power of *n*.

Your main battle, however, is with the one adversary who will never go away – yourself. For all but a few people, there's a gap between what they achieve and what they know they could (and often should) attain. To use a term from athletics, your ultimate PB (Personal Best) always lies somewhere beyond your AB (Actual Best). The quest for the PB begins with the *kaizen* of performance – continuous improvement. But beyond that lies *kaikaku*: the radical breakthrough that lifts your career and/or your company to a new and much higher plane.

One easily tapped source of breakthrough ideas is the bookshelf. Books (like this one) draw on the accumulated wisdom and experience of past and present, and throw in thought and analysis of the author's own, to propose new and more powerful approaches to the eternal tasks of management. Eternal is the word. Often the grand thoughts of the grand gurus prove to be repetitions of ancient truths: dressed up in new clothes, true; none the lower in value for that; but familiar advice all the same.

That observation applies both to impressive tomes like David Goleman's *Emotional Intelligence* (whoever thought that human feelings and interactions don't govern real-life management?); and small-sized works with giant-sized sales like *The One Minute Manager* (who hasn't heard its main teaching, which is on delegation, that you shouldn't get a dog and then bark yourself?).

Whether the wisdom is ancient or modern, the issue is not its value, but its use. For every Forrest Mars, who (as noted earlier) picked up his idiosyncratic ideas about business economics from a little-known book, there are numberless managers who never turn a page, or, having done so, never act on the ideas therein. Many managers, still worse, even pay for expensive advice that they fail to use. You need little motivation to pick up a book or phone a consultant. But to turn their teaching into personal value for you and your company, the motivation has to be truly high.

Pasquale Pistorio turned an also-ran semiconductor company, SGS-Thomson, into a European powerhouse, now renamed STMicroelectronics, after reading (twice) a seminal book titled *Kaizen* by Masaaki Imai. The Japanese master's words inspired Pistorio to adopt Total Quality Management as the driver he required to take an ill-fitting merger of French, Italian and British interests to the top rank of micro-electronics companies. Imai was the catalyst, but not the motivation; that lay in Pistorio's determination to overtake superior competitors.

Ψ

Competition has acquired a curious sanctity in the twenty-first century, thanks to its avid adoption by politicians both left and right, going right back to the future Baroness Thatcher. The underlying philosophy is that of the eighteenth century Scottish economist Adam Smith. Adapted to modern circumstances, the gospel holds that, in their worthy desire to outperform their rivals, companies will raise efficiency and lower prices, leading to great joy all round.

In pursuit of this ill-founded belief, the politicians established ersatz competition in places where it was impossible – for instance, the provision of healthcare; and blithely limited or lifted the restraints that earlier politicians had (wisely) invented to curb the inherent tendency of competitors to cheat – to maximize profits by minimizing the actual amount of competition. For example, mergers of competing firms, whatever else they do or don't achieve, hardly increase competition.

Where competition truly works is in motivation. The urge to outrace, outwrestle, outdo the other fellow is a powerful atavistic force in the human being. It helps visibly to give teams their binding force. It gives shape to objectives by providing an overall target to attack. It supplies benchmarks to measure comparative achievement and to drive the company towards best-of-breed status. It encapsulates pride, self-belief and positive thinking. It powers the pursuit of exciting ambitions.

In his last year (2004) at the helm of STM, Pistorio could proudly boast that his once-struggling company had become, with $7.24 billion of sales, 'the world-leading supplier of application-specific analog ICs [integrated circuits] overall with Number One rankings in various segments'. Number One has a magical resonance in any competition: who can ever forget a defiant Sebastian Coe raising one triumphant finger after winning the 1500m at the Los Angeles Olympics?

Sport is one of two areas that have a competitive affinity with management. The other, more familiar, is war. But while the military have contributed much to management, not least (for better or worse) the model for most corporate organizations, sport is the more relevant. For one thing, defeated armies rarely live to fight another day: sunken ships don't resurface: planes are shot down for keeps. But one race's beaten favourite can be the next race's unexpected champion, and vice versa.

Seb Coe demonstrated this truth at the previous Olympics in 1980, in Moscow. Unanimously backed by the experts to win the 800m (he held the world record),

Coe came second to fellow Brit Steve Ovett. Given no great chance in the 1500m, two-and-a-half days later, Coe won in superb style. In commercial markets, similar ups and downs happen all the time. For instance, Nokia seemed about to seize total control in mobile phones in 2003, having left rivals like Ericsson and Sony in its fast-moving wake: but, teamed together, the latter pair came back hard enough to cause Nokia acute discomfort in 2004.

The issue is not how to avoid setbacks, even calamities, in competitive environments. Such blows are bound to hurt from time to time. The test – for athlete and manager alike – is how you react to the emergency. In her climbing career Rebecca showed the necessary quality time and again: I call it 'grace under pressure', and regard its achievement as the moment of truth that shows the real quality of the individual – and the team. As I wrote with Will Carling, then a most successful England rugby captain, in *The Way to Win*:

'To non-athletes, the pressure of the putt that will win or lose the Open, the penalty that will win the Grand Slam [or the drop-kick that will win the World Cup], the serve on which the vital Wimbledon tie-break depends seems impossibly severe. To the champion it is just one more test of skill, concentration and preparation.'

Every athlete (and every manager) competes with himself or herself to achieve their personally supreme standards. But without competition that admirable effort has no objective and too little motivation. Competition sharpens the sword. In Coe's case, the 800m defeat was initially shattering. The damage was mental, not physical, so the mending could only take place in the mind. In the sixty hours between the two races, Coe turned to positive thinking. He reminded himself of all his past achievements, of the excellence of his racing skills and his athletic fitness. He *thought* himself back into the gold medal position.

Mental attitude is fundamental to winning. Think wrong, and you end up like O-mani, or Great Waves, a Japanese wrestler of universally admired physique and skill, but who never won a contest. O-mani approached a Zen master, who prescribed a night of meditation. 'Great Waves is your name ... Imagine that you are those billows. You are no longer a wrestler who is afraid. You are those huge waves, sweeping everything before them.' That evening, as described by Felix Rops in *Zen Flesh, Zen Bones*, the master left the wrestler in the temple. In the morning the *sensei* found the wrestler still meditating, 'with a faint smile on his face'. From then on, Great Waves won everything. He had become invincible.

There was something of the same aura about the great decathlon performer, Daley Thompson. Determined to lead the world's best, Thompson believes that he differed from other people in one critical mental respect: the thought that 'I'm good at it until proved otherwise'. Others, Thompson feels, think the opposite: that they will probably not be very good, but hope to be agreeably surprised. The same negative mindset often attributes far greater strength to the competition than it actually possesses.

Here lies a difficult balancing act. On the one hand, the manager needs the Thompson-like positivism that breeds decisive and fully committed action. On the other hand, managers also need (and badly) the realism of a well-found SWOT analysis. That accurately portrays their and the organization's Strengths; is no less objective about the Weaknesses; is painfully aware of all lost Opportunities; and, if anything (see above), exaggerates rather than underestimates the Threats emanating from the opposition.

Ψ

You could never have found a feistier or more self-confident manager than Andy Grove, the key driver of Intel's world-changing progress. His celebrated book title, *Only the Paranoid Survive*, wasn't Grove's original choice; he preferred something far less sexy about 'strategic inflection points' (see Chapter 8). But he genuinely believes that a paranoid fear of being beaten is an indispensable motivator; even though Intel's strategy of building an overwhelming share of the world's manufacturing capacity for microprocessors is all but invincible.

Intel's winner-takes-nearly-all policies gave it twelfth rank in the *Harvard Business Review*'s list of North America's top 'High-Growth Value Adders' (July–August 2004). This ranking provides one quite complex answer to a vital and hard question. If you're measuring yourself against the competition, what measure do you choose? The short answer is that no overall measure is appropriate. The size and growth of revenues, profits, profitability, and market share all paint parts of the picture, but there's no measure of their combined effect – with the possible exception, for public companies, of the share price.

That value looms very large in the *HBR* rankings. Calculations by the Wall Street firm Stewart Stern took a company's total rise in stock market value (Market Value Added) over 20 years and divided this number by the 2003 revenues. This produced 'a ratio that indicates efficiency at translating revenues into added shareholder value', on which the companies were duly ranked. To be sure that the companies were achieving profitable growth, Stewart Stern also ranked them by revenue expansion over 20 years, and added the two rankings together. Hence the table below:

NORTH AMERICAN HIGH-GROWTH VALUE ADDERS ($ billion)		
	Revenue Growth	MVA
1 General Electric	107.4	251.6
2 Wal-Mart	239.8	185.8
3 Altria Group	72.4	62.6
4 Home Depot	58.0	56.4
5 Microsoft	32.1	227.7
6 Exxon Mobil	158.2	114.1
7 IBM	49.0	96.5
8 Johnson & Johnson	35.9	101.1
9 Pfizer	41.4	77.1
10 Dell	35.4	80.4

I couldn't ask for a better text for a sermon on the unreality of conventional corporate comparisons. There's not even a casual relationship, and certainly not a causal one, between the growth in revenues and the billions added to the value of the shares. The connection is plainly random. As for being 'a ratio that indicates efficiency at translating revenues into added shareholder value', just how did the managements concerned perform this handy trick? The fact is that the share price is outside management's control – or, indeed, anybody's.

Shares rise for only one reason, because orders to buy outweigh orders to sell; and they fall for the opposite reason. There is, of course, a connection between the balance of buy-and-sell orders and the real events involving the company. The announcement of a takeover bid at a premium level is a clear-cut example. But the link with financial performance is fuzzy. A doubling of profits should unquestionably boost the value of the shares, but by how much? No man knows. The same question, with the same know-not answer, applies when profits halve. Defenestration of the entire board of directors, too, would unquestionably move the shares. Upwards or downwards?

There is one sure path out of this maze. Don't put the share price first. Not only is this quotation the one significant parameter outside management's control, but it is a deeply unsatisfactory target, anyway. It says nothing about competitive strength and success. It's as if the award of Olympic gold medals were determined, not by the fastest times run or the longest distances jumped, but by the applause of the crowd.

Moreover, a management that focuses, above all else, on the share price diverts attention from performance to spin, and from the future to the present. These swaps are not valuable, but highly damaging.

The vital indicators of competitive success or failure range from the quite blunt instrument of market share, which hides as much as it tells, to very precise numbers for physical performance, and to less precise but highly indicative subjective counts, like comparative levels of customer satisfaction or dissatisfaction. You can't ignore any aspect of performance. Rather, emulate the intensely positive spirit of Daley Thompson, who aimed to raise his performance in the ten events of the decathlon to the point where his worst result, in each event, was better than anyone else's best.

Obviously enough, that would guarantee victory. Be inspired by Thompson to run your own private decathlon. What are the ten key 'races' on which, first, your personal achievement and, second, that of the organization, depend? What are the best, most telling measures of performance? Can you use these yardsticks for meaningful comparisons with the performance of your competitors?

But there's another crucial question that must be asked. The individual and the organization need to know:

AM I COMPETING IN THE RIGHT EVENT?

- Is my present field the one that gives me the best chance of success?

- Does it provide the best use of my talents?

- Does it offer the highest level of those rewards that mean most to me?

- Does it provide the widest zone of opportunity?

- Will it bring me the desired level of recognition and fame?

The thinking behind this questionnaire is unarguable. If you pick a career or job that does not use your best abilities, you will inevitably underperform. You are excluding opportunities that, with equal inevitability, would have satisfied you far more. The questions, with 'we' substituted for the individual, apply just as strongly to business organizations. If you don't compete in the markets offering the highest growth and profitability, you cannot complain if your growth and profits lag behind the wiser competitors. Look at this second table from the *Harvard Business Review*:

EUROPEAN HIGH-GROWTH VALUE ADDERS ($ billion)		
	Revenue Growth	MVA
1 Nestlé	59.2	65.6
2 Total	92.4	83.5
3 GlaxoSmithKline	36.9	122.2
4 Eni	50.7	46.2
5 BP	185.5	102.3
6 Royal Dutch/Shell Group	124.8	89.5
7 Nokia	34.5	61.6
8 France Telecom	57.4	26.5
9 Deutsche Telekom	42.2	38.0
10 Telefónica	30.8	46.6

The above list consists of one food manufacturer, one pharmaceutical giant, one electronics champion, and one retailer. The others (three each) divide between energy and telecoms. The inference must be that European managers have not in general looked for or found outstanding success in innovative products. The contrast with the US (see page 138) is stark. The Top Ten Americans include just one energy company: there are two retailers (the mighty Wal-Mart and Home Depot) and one food manufacturer; but the remaining six are all leading-edge manufacturers.

Their businesses take in computer software, hardware and services; pharmaceuticals; and aerospace (jet engines being one of GE's multifarious activities). Against this scintillating array, the Europeans look downright dull – as do their results. Their average revenue growth over the two decades to 2003 was $71.4 billion. That's within touching distance of the $83 billion averaged by the Americans (both figures being artificially boosted by acquisitions). However, Europe's growth champions added Market Value of only $68.2 billion, little more than half the $125.3 billion for the US Top Ten.

Another notable lead of the Americans is in corporate youth, which naturally goes hand-in-hand with innovation and leading-edge technology. Wal-Mart, Home Depot, Microsoft and Dell are all children of the late twentieth century – Home Depot was barely born in 1983. Only one of the Europeans qualifies on this count – Nokia, an old company radically remade. The Finnish maestro of the mobile phone also shares an American penchant for sideways competition – the best kind there is. Only a fool, a brave one, but a fool nevertheless, tackles entrenched and powerful competition head-on. So go round the side!

Ψ

Nokia won its lead over rival makers of telecommunication equipment by concentrating all its resources on the single front of mobile phones. Microsoft removed IBM from its field of play by winning the invaluable freedom to sell its MS-DOS operating system to all comers. Michael Dell zoomed to the top of the PC market by selling direct to customers, leaving far more powerful competitors like IBM and Compaq burdened by middlemen. Sam Walton built Wal-Mart to gigantic size by opening his discount stores in nondescript, smaller towns that the opposition powers had neglected – and went on neglecting.

Here lies another advantage of going round the side: the rich, complacent competition very probably won't compete with a sideways upstart until far too late. That delay is an expensive hobby; and its success is by no means guaranteed. Thus, IBM spent untold billions on an operating system intended to knock Microsoft off its perch, only to see the little challenger swell hugely, riding on the back of Windows 3, and storming far ahead of IBM in market value.

The giant-killing manoeuvre is called left or right flanking by the military, who nearly always win their battles by going round the side. In fact, according to B.H. Liddell Hart, whose researches started from the ancient Greeks and ended with the First World War, out of six major conflicts and 280 campaigns, only six achieved decisive results by full frontal assault.

Philip Kotler and Ravi Singh enumerate three other alternatives to sideways assault: encirclement, bypass attack and guerrilla warfare. But all three, on closer examination, are really variations on the main choice between flanking and frontal assault. The authors themselves warn, for example, against putting too much trust in guerrilla war: selective price cuts, raiding the enemy's supply lines, poaching key employees, and sudden and savage promotional attacks will all irritate the competitor no end, but they won't vanquish him.

Only a much stronger attack will do that – very probably by flanking, very improbably by frontal confrontation. Kotler and Singh reckon that you require a three-to-one advantage for the latter to succeed. Even then, you're probably wasting frontal effort. In the first Gulf War, the Allies may well have enjoyed at least a three-to-one advantage over the effective (or ineffective) strength of Saddam Hussein's forces: but General 'Stormin Norman' Schwarzkopf still opted for a huge left hook through the desert, outflanking and duly routing his shattered opponents.

The trench warfare of the First World War provides another instructive metaphor. When heavyweight companies play by the same rules, adopt the same strategies, and indulge in the same types of mergers and acquisitions, their competition is strictly nominal, and deadlock follows. Like those crafty American growth champions in the table, the true competitor dodges deadlock, but thinks positively and strives for the winning difference and the louder bang per buck of expenditure.

This kind of competition rests on innovation in all things – not products alone, but all processes, especially those involving the intellectual contribution of people at all levels. Out-thinking and outflanking go hand-in-hand. Given great ideas, greatly implemented, you can climb the highest, coldest and windiest mountains – and do so before anyone else.

SUMMIT 6

- Exploit the great power of **positive thinking** to reinforce your inherent desires.

- Outdo the competition by the strength of your **ambition** and the thoroughness of your **preparation**.

- Told that something is too **difficult**, even impossible, think 'for you maybe, but **not** necessarily **for me**'.

- Develop **mutual trust**, based on understanding, as the team's secret competitive weapon.

- Let the **managed** themselves **form** the demanding, stretching **expectations** that lead to **triumph**.

- Regard **adversity** as your **chance** to test and hone the essential quality of 'grace under pressure'.

- Remember that **victories** are **won**, and defeats suffered, in the **mind**: think victory!

- Base competition on realistic **knowledge** of your Strengths, Weaknesses, Opportunities and Threats.

- **Don't** tackle established competition **head–on**: go round the **side**!

- Compete only in contests that best use **your talents** and offer the **best** potential **outcomes**.

Never Letting Up 1

VINSON MASSIF, 4,897M (16,066FT)

Named after Carl G.Vinson, a US congressman and an important figure in promoting Antarctic exploration, Vinson is situated in the southern half of the Sentinel Range that, with the Heritage Range, makes up the Ellsworth Mountains, home to most of Antarctica's highest peaks. The last of the Seven Summits to be discovered and climbed, it was only spotted in 1957, by US Navy pilots, and climbed for the first time in 1966 by a US expedition from the National Geographic Society, the American Alpine Club and the National Science Foundation. It is a massif rather than a mountain, 13 miles long and eight miles wide, situated at 78°S, some 750 miles from the South Pole. It is a technically straightforward climb, but the hostile, unforgiving climate makes it a serious undertaking.

Vinson was the last of my Seven Summits and although remote and as cold as any mountain in the world, it is otherwise a straightforward climb and, by comparison with Aconcagua, diminutive. A successful completion of the Seven Summits was virtually in the bag – the only danger ahead of me, complacency.

The learning process is never complete, however, even when the end of a project is within sight. On Aconcagua it had been drummed into me just how important it is to have a self-reliant, trusting team, especially when things get tough – yet on Vinson I was going to be alone among strangers. For reasons of cost I had planned to fly to Antarctica on my own and meet up with a guided expedition on Vinson. Now I realized the error of my judgement. If I was to climb as part of this guided expedition and the weather was bad – as extreme, say, as we'd just experienced on Aconcagua – then the decision as to whether or not to climb would be taken by a guide who I didn't know, and, as important, didn't know me. With safety in mind, a guide ignorant of his or her clients' capabilities would quite rightly decide, 'no, it simply isn't worth the risk.'

I was playing this over in my mind as we paced hurriedly from the base camp of Aconcagua to the road head, to pick up transport to Santiago. I couldn't help but think how much more satisfactory it would be if one of my fellow climbers could accompany me to Antarctica, so that I could climb as a part of a self-contained team – and talked it over with the three of them. John and Barny, it turned out, had commitments at home, but Dave was as free as the air. By the time we approached our sponsor's office in Santiago (DHL is a good sponsor, in that it has offices in every major city around the world) our minds were made up. Dave would climb with me on Vinson. The only obstacle was money. To fly an additional person to Vinson would cost a princely $25,000.

Unsurprisingly, the staff at DHL Santiago were in no position to authorize this money. They did, however, have a telephone directory of every company employee in the world, listing both their work extension numbers and their numbers at home, which they gave to me. It was 6.00 p.m. in Santiago, 10.00pm in London – and I called the UK Chairman, David Allen, at home. He was out. I picked up the phone again, this time to call the Managing Director Nick Butcher. Lucky this time; he picked up the phone and I began to explain our predicament. 'Mr Butcher,' I said, 'if we want the best chance of success we really need one of the Aconcagua team to join me in Antarctica, and ... (pause) ... that's going to cost $25,000.'

'Call it done,' he said. He didn't hesitate, adding that he felt quite sure we understood the circumstances in which we found ourselves far better than he ever could.

'And by the way,' he added, 'my name is Nick,' and put the phone down.

I could barely take on board his generosity, not to mention his extremely touching trust of our judgement.

Ψ

The very next morning, Dave and I flew to Punta Arenas – a dusty town of tireless winds at the very foot of Chile's elongated body – and there boarded a Hercules and flew across the Southern Ocean to a runway of compacted blue ice in the snowy wastelands of Antarctica. We stepped off the back of the Hercules and immediately were immersed in an intense, unfiltered Antarctic sunlight – this at 3 o'clock in the morning – and slipped and slid the couple of hundred metres to Patriot Hills, a temporary encampment established only in the short summer season for those starting their various adventures in Antarctica.

From here we flew again, forty minutes or so, in a Twin Otter this time, to the base of the Vinson Massif. This was wilderness in its truest form – snow, ice, sky, mountains, exquisitely serene, and, once the plane had fired its engines and departed, empty. The freedom of it all jolted me alive.

I shouldn't forget to mention that Ginette wasn't on the flight. We had a clear run ahead of us and it was difficult to imagine how we could fail. Just off Aconcagua, we were well-acclimatized to the altitude and Vinson was, by all accounts, a mountain free of major obstacles. The climb should take about five days.

Still, we couldn't afford to lose focus. This was Antarctica, the coldest continent on Earth. It was November, early summer in the southern hemisphere. Come the evening and the sun didn't set below the far horizon, but it did slump behind the surrounding hills – and the ensuing drop in temperature had us scurrying to our sleeping bags. So frigid was the air, that come the morning, I didn't dare reach out a hand to light the stove, or reach for a book, but just lay there, cocooned in my sleeping bag from my toes to the crown of my head, waiting for the sun to hit our tent. 'Cold as I've ever known it', one regular to the Antarctic said.

However, with the exception of a couple of days when a heavy fall of snow had us pinned in our tents, everything went to plan. Day 7 and we walked the length of a high cwm and up a steeply inclined face onto the summit ridge. The mountain was bathed in brilliant sunshine. Dave was ahead of me. I took a last few paces and stepped on top of Vinson's summit – and burst into tears. Such a rush of joy, and relief. The view from the top was so splendidly rare and lovely: the purest white snow – untainted – stretching as far as we could see, with just the very tops of a scattering of mountains protruding above the vertical miles of glacial ice, like islands in a frozen sea. I wanted to jump in a boat and sail to them.

And the relief? For a number of years I had lived with the uncertainty that I would ever complete this project. On Vinson's summit, that day in November 1994, doubt faded away ... thanks to my climbing companions, and the Sherpas, and our sponsors, and my family for not being petrified with concern, and a good run of luck that kept both impossibly dangerous weather and poor health at bay.

But in the mix of joy and relief there was an emptiness, too, for it was all over. An all-consuming, magical period of my life was at an end, and the question was now, 'what's next?'

REFLECTIONS

Don't let up until the very end – that was Vinson's lesson. Even on the home straight we must be prepared to invest time, energy and resources if we want to ensure success.

It was important, too, to realize that the project wasn't over just because the Seventh Summit had been climbed. On my return to London, there were multiple sponsorship obligations to meet, as well as a pile of thank you letters as high as a minor peak to write and deliver. It might have been tempting to overlook these duties and move on to whatever project was next, but that would have been a mistake, not only because it would have failed those who had made our venture a success, but also because in this world we live on our reputation, and a failure to tidy up the loose ends of one project might well lead to failure in the initiation of another.

Which leads me on to the big question – what next? After climbing the Seven Summits, I'll confess that all I wanted to do was to lie on a beach! Time, please, to do nothing, other than dabble a big toe in some warm water! But after a period of recuperation my thoughts naturally turned to what might lie in the future. And, it appeared, other people's thoughts turned to this question as well.

'So what's next?' friends would ask. Or, if they were mountaineers, 'How about K2?'

At 8,611m, K2 is 235m lower than Everest but more challenging in every other regard. I had never wanted to climb K2, though – even had I thought I was able. The relationship I had with it was very different from the one I had with Everest. With the latter I had fallen in love – with its history, its people and the landscape surrounding it. K2 I had never laid eyes on, and the stories I'd heard about it from friends who had ventured onto its treacherous slopes were all touched with gloom and tragedy. It's a very dangerous mountain.

Yet we're an impressionable lot. So many people asked me the question that eventually I turned it on myself: 'What about K2?' Could I imagine myself climbing its upper slopes and standing on its rarely-trodden summit?

Almost as quickly as I asked myself the question I realized the answer was 'no'. What was I thinking? This wasn't something that I wanted to do. It wasn't a desire that sprang, like new life, from within me. Without the will to do it, I realized, I would barely be able to summon the enthusiasm to walk to the base camp. And what if, like so many climbers on K2, I didn't make it home? It would be a sad waste of life if it wasn't my own star I was following but someone else's.

No thank you. In my quieter moments I realized how fortunate I was to be alive, and the Seven Summits, far from satisfying my ambition, only served to widen my horizons. There were, and are, many more mountains to climb, both real and metaphorical, and now, more than ever, I understand the need to follow my own convictions.

Never Letting Up 2

In management and on mountains, persistence is a virtue. Good climbers hate to let go. If at first they don't succeed, they try, try again. If they do succeed, they try even harder. Rebecca could have climbed Everest and then abandoned her pursuit of mountaineering firsts; instead she perceived and seized the opportunity to complete the Grand Tour of the Seven Summits.

Approaching the Seventh of these, Mount Vinson, an Antarctic midget of 4,897m (16,066ft), she could have taken its conquest for granted. To make doubly sure, though, she recruited an extra climber. Even when victory looks assured, always be ready to invest more time, effort and money to ensure success. You don't let up until the very end – and you act as if that end will never arrive.

The mighty Konosuke Matsushita celebrated the golden jubilee of his colossal enterprise at a company conference, where he noted that the last fifty years had been quite successful. Now, he demanded, what about the next fifty? He was in his own eighties at the time. Keeping right on to the end of the road, and then beyond, seems to come naturally to the Japanese mind – another Japanese company once ran an ad campaign celebrating 'The First 2,000 Years of Hitachi'.

Western managers, though, are often great ones for giving up. They launch many and varied 'initiatives' and institute all manner of 'programmes' for improvement, then abandon the new and wonderful cause long before meaningful results could have appeared. Institutional change takes more time and persistence than many managers are prepared to offer. But if you're paying more than lip-service to customer service excellence, for example, you really are embarking on a voyage without end.

According to Jacques Horovitz, the expert who helped to make Club Mediterranée a byword for service wonders, you need a decade to build excellent service standards (the only ones worth having) into the organization's way of life. Horovitz is adamant about the ten years; 'after that it's irreversible. If you don't take ten years, it's reversible'. But many such change programmes run out of steam and sponsorship in ten months. They don't die. They are slain by mismanagement.

Change managers, to be fair, face two built-in difficulties. First, they not only need the ringing endorsement of senior managers, above all the CEO, but their active participation. Yet CEOs come and go: and with them, all too often, go their pet projects. Even if the bosses stay, their enthusiasm may fade, overtaken by other priorities. There are, after all, so many areas of any business that need major improvement. Which of them do you choose?

The short answer is that, compared with an activist CEO, Hercules had it easy. He only had the endlessly filthy Augean stables to clean. To all intents and purposes, a business has an infinite series of interlocking Augean challenges. You dare not concentrate on any one at the expense of the others – not even customer service. Club Mediterannée didn't lose its leadership in European tourism because its service quality slipped. The failure was strategic. The company had become hard-wired to a particular way of serving a holiday market that had fundamentally changed.

Persistence with a commitment to quality like the Club's is splendid. But strategic decision-making is just as much a management process as dealing with customer complaints. Strategy, though, is reserved to the managerial upper class, which rarely accepts that its methods can be investigated, let alone improved. These seniors are not the only managers who persist with failure. The instinctive human reaction is to leave well alone – a philosophy enshrined in the timeworn phrase: 'If it ain't broke, don't fix it'.

Ψ

The trouble is that you may actually be leaving bad alone. An astonishing phenomenon of the new millennium was the way in which former idols of British retail management, living through a period of sustained growth in consumer spending, fell out of favour with everybody, and into financial decline. The customers certainly saw what was 'broke' at Marks & Spencer, J Sainsbury, Boots and WHSmith. But too much of the breakage wasn't fixed, largely because managements failed to share, or to act on, the critical perceptions of customers and other outsiders.

What you think about yourself and your organization is unlikely to be wholly true, or even relevant. The real relevance lies in the perceptions of others. You may feel that these perceptions are deeply mistaken. That misses the point entirely. You have to deal with the sovereign reality of the perceptions themselves. If the perceptions are right, you must change what is wrong. If the perceptions are wrong, you must seek to right them – and that's the harder task.

Western managers and gurus hamper their efforts to improve by a tendency to fasten on supposed fast-working panaceas. In contrast, the east thinks long-term and evolutionary – as in Lean Management. This is the philosophy and practice of continually cutting costs by eliminating waste (*muda* in Japanese) in ways that also save time. The extraordinary results are detailed in an enthusiastic book entitled *Kaikaku*, by Norman Bodek – who describes 'lean' as follows:

'The Power and Magic of Lean is to discover those hidden treasures in your company: to find and eliminate all of the non-value-adding wastes and to bring out the infinite creative capacity from every single worker'.

The book's title is somewhat misleading, since *kaikaku* means 'radical change', though most of Bodek's examples demonstrate the power and magic of *kaizen*, or 'continuous improvement'. But the impact of 'lean' can be so forceful that it truly adds up to revolution. The English plant of Heinz, for example, faced a sorely besetting problem in meeting orders from Tesco and Sainsbury's for own-label tomato ketchup. Heinz took four hours to change the line over from its own brand. Mountains of inventory were needed, and profits suffered.

The engineers were put to work. They cut the changeover time from four hours, not by half, or even three-quarters, but by over 96% to a mere eight minutes. They owed this stunning success to the work of Dr Shigeo Shingo, the hero of Bodek's book, and the man who shares credit with the fabled Taiichi Ohno for the Toyota Production System – the spiritual and practical home of 'lean'.

Shingo's *modus operandi* couldn't be more direct; take the 'five whys', a true working model of persistence. If somebody comes to you with a problem, ask 'Why?' the problem has arisen. You don't let up when you have your answer. You go on asking 'Why?' until you have uncovered the root cause of the trouble. Five 'Whys' will nearly always do the trick.

Bodek gives the example of soldering misconnects. Shingo wanted to know why these occurred. Answer: 'Well, sometimes the solder doesn't melt properly'. Second question: 'Why does that happen?' asked the guru (or *sensei*). It took two more 'whys' for an engineer to come up with the root cause, to which a solution instantly appeared (as it often will, once the problem is correctly defined).

Managers unversed in the principles of 'lean', even if they ask the first 'Why?' (often and sadly neglected), are too easily satisfied and don't persist with the magic word to the equally magical conclusion. The crucial point that leaps out from the 'five whys' is that 'lean' isn't merely a matter of technical know-how (although that is crucial), but that human interactions and people management are even more important.

Ψ

W. Edwards Deming, the American who transformed Japanese industry post-war by introducing the magic of Statistical Quality Control, was no dry-as-dust scientist, but a humanitarian. He believed profoundly in the ability of people to exercise initiative and improve their performance – if only the system could be stopped from getting in their way. The better the workplace, the better would be its management and encouragement of people.

Thus, the master Shingo nominated a Matsushita washing machine plant as the world's best, so Bodek paid a visit. Of the fifteen features that distinguished the plant, the first two were strictly humanist: 'people were encouraged to continuously improve their skills and utilize their energy'; and 'people's personal lives and well-being were always considered through athletic programmes and job enrichment activities'.

Likewise, the Toyota Production System, when attacking waste with vim and vigour, lists among the specific, sane and successful technical advice (like 'cutting down on the distance things move throughout the plant') some very broad and humane recommendations – above all, 'utilize the inherent talent of your workers'. They won't be using that talent if they are kept waiting around, looking impotently at idle machines, or made to spend hours on changeovers that take Matsushita minutes. That's the result of another potent cause of waste: 'Not managing properly'.

There is no advantage for anybody in managing improperly; especially when the proper alternative makes your life and the lives of all your people easier – much easier, and more profitable. If the present nature and standards of management are appropriate and effective – because you never let up – you can build on ideas strong enough to create your future: the one you and your colleagues want for yourselves.

Creating your own future demands narrowing the ever-present gap between generating ideas (imaginative creativity) and achieving results (executive creativity). That also means closing the yawning divide between the typical organization's current behaviours and those that foster the creation and execution of excellent ideas. That is something that managers generally find unnecessarily difficult. The system, which should be designed to support and speed 'ideation', instead undermines and blocks its vital processes.

To break the problem, crack the organizational mould. Here, for example, are what I diagnosed as ten prime mould-breaking attributes of an ace high-tech supplier: ARM, designer of 75% of the silicon chips used in mobile phones. ARM was one of three companies that I visited in the summer of 2004, commissioned by the East of England Development Agency to conduct 'ideas audits'. How did this trio go about finding, developing and implementing ideas? The following ten questions, all of which ARM can answer positively, provide a concise guide to MPS (Management for Persistent Success).

1   Have you got the business model right – and will you keep it that way?

2   Do you make the customers into real and treasured partners in the business?

3   Do you honour and reward the innovators?

4   Do you foster – and never lose – a burning desire to survive and succeed?

5   Do you constantly develop new ideas to attack new markets?

6   Does R&D have its own special place in the organization?

7   Do you ensure a proper balance between current development and further-out, future research?

8   Do you make sure that there's a place and hearing for wacky and far-out thinking?

9   Are closely knit teams of people created for all activities?

10   Do you regard challenges as the source of the best opportunities – and willingly accept them?

Would any of those policies strain *your* organization? Do you consider any of them wrong-headed, or dangerous? Are they approaches that can ever be let go? Surely, the ten are not only evidently practical and beneficial; they constitute part of the template for the Ideas Company, the only kind that can create its own future. But there's another question, of course: how many of the ten actually feature in the management of your own workplace?

My educated guess is that very few established companies practise more than one or two of these ten behaviours – any one of which will wither away without long-term persistence. Misfiring managements, however, even if they acknowledge the case for the ten ARM attributes, pay them only lip-service. They may have a business model, for instance, but it will be much the same as the competition's, providing no useful edge, let alone a transcendent one.

Despite many fine words about customer relations, these are often antagonistic – and short-term at that (see Horovitz of Club Méditerranée, above). The misfiring firms may talk about innovation, too, but practice lags far behind, and the innovators get little special recognition or reward. Yes, their employers think unorthodox thought and thinkers to be important – but both are ignored. The managements do desire to survive, of course, but they fall back into defensive strategies that militate against outstanding success. And if meeting the challenge involves disruptive action (as it certainly will), *that* is delayed as long as possible – too long – and so on.

ARM's credo is the reverse of these traditional failings. True, ARM is a grown-up, high-tech start-up that doesn't have the historical lumber or organizational deadweight that hamper businesses of greater age and with slower-moving technology and markets. But weren't the gee-whiz digital growth stars supposed to become the models for all businesses in the twenty-first century? Of course, many stars were nothing like their inflated, over-hyped reputations. But their speed of reaction and innovation was and is real enough. And that speed is in itself useful armour against the unexpected: i.e., the future.

If you're heading in the wrong direction, the faster you can turn about, the better. But ARM's ever-urgent need for organized haste isn't shared by all companies. I visited one company far distant from ARM. It is old-established (born in 1876), sells a most traditional product (English ale), and, unlike the global ARM, is mainly confined to one area, the East of England. Where ARM is a public company that has been riding the high-tech seesaw, the brewer, Charles Wells, is private and family-owned.

As for the future; not long ago Wells seemed to have none. Giants were mopping up the independent breweries. So what behaviours have kept the company thriving, growing and independent? Again, there are ten questions to ask and answer:

1   Do you base new development on a foundation of lasting and relevant virtues?

2   Is continuous improvement over time used as the basis for radical change?

3   Does everybody act to build the brand – meaning both the corporate brand and the products?

4   Are you old-fashioned about good financial housekeeping and strategic prudence?

5   Are you innovatory about everything else, with new projects at all levels and in all activities?

6   Do you shun insistence on being first – but very much insist on being best?

7   Are you very patient but extremely determined in breaking new ground?

8   Do you keep close to the customers and develop new ideas around satisfying their needs?

9   Are all staff fully involved in the company's strategy and its progress?

10   Is there a unifying and bold ambition to which everybody can respond?

On that tenth point, Wells is unlikely to rest until at least one of its beers is on sale in every outlet in Britain. But all ten questions, for most companies, are as hard to answer with an honest Yes as the queries governing ARM as it pursues an ambition of Microsoft qualities. Ambition apart, there are self-evident differences in flavour between ARM and the Wells brand of enlightened conservatism – as you would expect, given the differences in the markets, products, ownership and history.

That difference itself propounds an undeniable truth. My recent book, *The Fusion Manager*, put this across emphatically. Much as managers would love to find the one right answer, none exists: the right answer is whatever best fits your individual circumstances at the right time. As the circumstances change, so will the right response. Neither ARM nor Wells is run by theorists, but, rather, they share an essential pragmatism – and a driving persistence (of which Charles Wells is a true model).

Yet there is a valuable place for theory and experiment. At HFL, my third study, the astonishing aim is to create 'The Perfect Company' – an objective stated in full awareness of the state of the art (or arts) of management. The aim is, of course, impossible, since perfection is available to few humans – and certainly not to companies. The pursuit of perfection, though, is another matter: eminently feasible, and terrific as an animating, dynamic force.

The bedrock of HFL's business doesn't look dynamic at first sight. Its people work in bioanalysis, primarily the testing of racehorse and greyhound body samples to check that no illegal substances have been used to enhance the animal's performance. Since scientific perfection actually is a realistic pursuit, the work is a good match for HFL's ceaseless and many-sided search for perfect corporate performance. The ten key principles I found there lead to vigorous and vital questions:

1   Do you set all targets and ambitions at the highest feasible pitch?

2   Do you use every known channel of internal communication, and invent ones of your own?

3   Do you make voluntary activity a critical element in running an ideas organization?

4   Do you use IT – e-mail and intranet – as a positive means of storing and exchanging ideas?

5   Do you lead from the top, but to animate and facilitate, not to command and control?

6   Do you relate all innovatory activities to the strategy and economic performance of the business?

7   Do you look for new ideas in management and people policies, and not only in products and processes?

8   Do you use informal methods to reinforce the formal elements of the organization?

9   Are you never shy about 'creative swiping' – borrowing and adapting from other companies?

10 Do you invest in people's personal as well as their professional development?

As noted, this list is more avant-garde than those at ARM or Charles Wells: yet it's hard to believe that the other two managements could not subscribe to the HFL policies. Investing in your staff's personal development is clearly a sound, indeed, unarguable idea, for instance. So is the stress on communication, and the openness to new ideas in all departments. So is making the intranet into the digital lifeblood of the business. The emphases differ between the different companies, as they must: but all three sing from the same hymn sheet.

Ψ

Recognizing the high value of these thirty questions, and of the policies they embody, is one thing, however. Putting the policies into action is quite another. For a start, who is the 'you' in the questions? Only a chief executive is in any position to demand and pursue the required action on all points. But there's much that other 'yous' can do, even if 'you' lack any real authority. You do not, after all, have to accept organizational behaviour that 'you' believe to be wrong.

It's gap-closing that's at issue again – closing the usual gulf between what people know to be right and the wrong things that actually happen: between good intentions and inadequate, or even absent execution.

You may feel that the pressures of business, let alone hierarchy, leave no room or time or possibility for all these desirable deeds. But the future will not wait for you or your organization to catch up.

If you are barred from helping to create a better company, and never mind a perfect one, be prepared to seek another corporate mountain to climb. The possible peaks are innumerable – and these three companies demonstrate that forward-looking, firmly based management is not the prerogative of large groups. The biggest of the three, ARM, has 750 employees; Charles Wells has half that total, 365; HFL is half of Wells. Size, whether big, middling or small, is no barrier to persisting in *three crucial policies*, which all depend on that precious quality of intelligent persistence:

- Unreasonably high ambitions, shared by everybody.

- People-centric management, pervading all policies and processes.

- Determination to build your respective Ten Commandments into the fabric of the organization -'the way we do things round here'.

Persistence comes in because the Crucial Trio cannot be installed overnight. When you embark on the creation of a company fit for the future, you are looking, as with creating true customer focus, a whole ten years ahead. In other words, you are committing the whole organization to attitudes and approaches that are designed to achieve effective change deep into the New Millennium. That isn't uncertain futurology, it's certain: 'it's the way we're going to do things round here' – for ever.

- Invest more **time**, **effort** and **money** to ensure **success** even when victory looks assured.

- **Tidy up** the loose ends of one project **before** going on to the next.

- Keep right on to the **very end** of the road – and then **beyond**.

- Follow **your own star** rather than the expectations of others.

- Apply the principles of Lean Management, **cutting out waste** of time and money, to everything you do

- **Encourage** people to continuously **improve** their skills and optimize their use of energy.

- **Strive** persistently to **close the gap** between what people know to be **right** and the **wrong** things that actually happen.

- Form unreasonably **high** long-term **ambitions** – and **share** them with everybody.

- Make management people-centric, putting **people at the centre** of all policies and processes.

- Draw up **your own Ten Commandments** and build them into the fabric of the organization – 'the way we do things round here'.

Playing the Encore

Even Seven-Summit successes – managers and organizations alike – run out of steam. In Rebecca's case, she ran out of summits (not being interested in conquering the fearsome K2). But a new career beckoned, in passing on her hard-won experience and expertise to others. Career change is one way of continuing the climb. Another, paradoxically, is to step back, to leave others to carry on the operational work under your benign but watchful eye.

The first Rockefeller both stepped back *and* found a new occupation. In his fifties, he passed executive control to his hand-picked associates and turned to philanthropy on a grand scale for the next four decades. What's needed at the base of the First Summit is required at all subsequent stages. You need to work out what you want (the Purpose) and how you will win that great prize (the Plan). Again, you need to assess where you are now, and what you must achieve, step by step, to get where you want to be.

The key lesson of the Seven Summits of Success is that the upward climb is one that anyone can achieve and enjoy. Getting to the heights, above all, requires the will to make that thrilling and rewarding ascent. But will that climb be enough? Even people of self-evident success end their lives, not luxuriating in their achievements, but regretting lost opportunities and unrealized ambitions. The great game has to end eventually, however. Sooner or later, by the intervention of God or man, or by the individual's own choice, retirement will beckon.

Business organizations, though, seldom retire. On the contrary, they are supposed to grow and prosper into an infinite future. So much for supposition. In point of fact, organizations do dwindle and even disappear. Any comparison of leading companies of different eras reveals a large number of big-name drop-outs. This may be misleading, since many vanish into mergers, and the businesses may survive intact in the new corporate shell. More likely, such survivors will be lesser powers, living (or half-alive) proof that success creates its own difficulties.

The most hazardous of these problems is expressed in a familiar question. What do I do for an encore? The question mainly arises in business if your mine runs out of gold. Or, to change metaphors, if you've climbed the highest mountains – and there are, by definition, none higher to scale.

Literally, as opposed to metaphorically, that happened to Rebecca. As noted above, she could have assaulted K2, the difficult and dangerous mountain that ranks second only to Everest in height. But this wasn't a challenge that gripped Rebecca, and wasn't part of her personal vision. So she set about building a new career, in which lecturing to groups of managers has grown increasingly important.

This book in part grew out of those lectures. Rebecca speaks to these audiences about her climbs and relates her experiences on the Seven Summits to the lives and work of her audience. The analogy applies both to them as people and to the business, for careers peak as well as markets. Then, the instinctive reaction of the careerist is to soldier on. But that must usually mean condemning yourself and/or the business to a process of diminishing returns.

The path chosen by Rebecca is far wiser: to strike out in a new direction, to launch a second life. The necessity that afflicts corporations, and sometimes individuals, has been brilliantly described by two very different experts on management – Charles Handy, the British writer and management philosopher, and Andrew S. Grove, one of the few top managers to have written a serious and original book on management – in fact, two of them; *High Output Management* and the better known *Only the Paranoid Survive.*

Grove's belief in paranoia is deeply understandable, since his company, Intel, nearly went under as the Japanese assault on its business in memory chips drove the company to the wall. Memories were Intel's core, an industry that it had created and long dominated. But the Japanese made these devices better and cheaper. In what then became a commodity market, Intel couldn't make a profit, no matter how hard a brilliant management strived.

As described in The First Summit, the market and Intel had reached what Grove later called a 'strategic inflection point'. That happens when change in the technology or other factors dramatically alters the name of the game. The consequences can be shown by what Handy identifies as a 'Sigmoid Curve'. It maps the life story of a company as it starts up, goes through the difficult early period of growth, overcomes the growing pains and then enjoys the periods (often many of them) in which sales and profits boom handsomely along.

But the golden days are numbered. At Point A on the Curve, still well below the coming peak, the writing is already on the wall. But customarily, nobody reads the message. Profitability is still marvellous, the shareholders are delighted, the customers are happy, the market is still strong. But inexorably the business moves on from Point A, rounds the heights of the Curve, and heads remorselessly downwards.

Look no further than the airlines for demonstrations of the Sigmoid trauma. The industry has been camped below Point B, on the downside of the Curve, for so long that only greybeards recall its former easy riches. As in the airlines, the efforts of management to return to the upside of the Curve are typically vitiated by financial losses, poor publicity, intense competition, consequent pressure on margins, and poor staff morale, which only weakens further with each successive wave of job cuts.

Ψ

Individual careers may not appear to follow such a curve. Looking back, successful careerists tend to see a straight upward line, marked at intervals by a new peak of achievement, another summit. But the career curve is real nonetheless. There are plateaus and hiatuses. Ends and means both sometimes have to change. The careerist can run into the equivalent of a strategic inflection point, when making a fresh start is not just desirable, but mandatory.

Comebacks, however, don't come easily, to individuals or organizations. Heavyweight boxers, it was said before Muhammad Ali changed the rules, never came back. Heavyweight companies still remain in a pre-Ali fix. They seldom return to their former power and glory – that is, if they continue to fight the same battle. That sorry truth is demonstrated by a book I wrote in 1987, *The State of Industry*. Based on broadcast interviews, it dealt with seventeen companies selected because of their stirring comebacks from a severe Thatcher recession.

The stories and the short-term results were convincing enough at the time. But the long-term outcome, all those years on, is fairly lamentable. Of the seventeen, only three can still be called strong survivors of their management wars and global leaders in their industries: Glaxo (now top dog at pharma giant GSK), Rolls-Royce in jet engines, and BOC in industrial gasses. Unable to achieve lasting profitable growth

SEVEN SUMMITS OF SUCCESS

from their existing activities, the others failed to win new growth from new ventures – from encores.

Grove at Intel was wiser and luckier. Deep in the company's bowels an engineer named Ted Hoff had set the new ball rolling with a revolutionary idea: instead of supplying a 'chip set' of separate components to electronics companies, why not place all the circuits on a single silicon wafer? Such a device could be programmed – and thus was born the microprocessor, the computer on a chip; the tiny foundation on which the entire digital revolution came to rest.

Intel's encore created a new megastar industry for itself and its customers and allies (not least Microsoft). Its escape from the Sigmoid threat provides a blueprint for the return to Point A – in Intel's case from well below Point B. The catechism for would-be encore managements is very demanding and applies equally to their companies and to individual managers and other careerists. (For the organization, simply substitute 'company' for 'you' and 'your'.)

1   Is the new venture within your established zones of competence and marketing know-how?

2   Will you change your *modus vivendi* radically – and fast enough – to exploit the encore opportunity?

3   Is the encore opportunity larger, and faster-growing in prospect, than your existing marketplace?

4   Do you have, or can you readily obtain, the talents required to take you in the new direction?

5   Can you take the encore activity to Point A – and beyond, to a whole series of new encores?

It's not hindsight alone that leads to the conclusion that both Andy Grove and Intel were uniquely equipped, at all five points, to seize the opportunity; to leave the now commoditized memory market to the Japanese; and to pioneer new frontiers. It was, of course, an all or nothing bet – to succeed or die. Such bets should in principle be avoided. But it's desperately hard to expect organizations, or individuals for that matter, to attack their whole beings, at a time of prosperity and success, to grasp a future that is by definition problematic.

The effort must be made, all the same. My associates at the Global Future Forum are intellectual mountaineers whose task is to think deeply about the new ranges that loom in the clouds ahead, or which may loom, and to work out the consequent scenarios that look likeliest to succeed. You can't predict the future – that gift is a human delusion – but you can *think* about the future, intelligently and in full possession of all relevant facts about the present.

Nobody pretends that these are easy exercises. But the amazingly foolish errors of the past do not, by and large, arise from misreading the future. The perpetrators haven't read the runes at all. Often, they ignored what was plain to see in the present. Would you, for example, have made all or any of the following hideously expensive errors about the shape of things to come?

- The rise in second-car families in the US as women went out more to work was obvious to the Japanese, but not to the American rivals – who also missed the significance of the large sales of VW's small Beetles.

- All IBM's competitors missed the fact, clear from the rise of Apple, that PCs were creating an entirely new computing market of fabulous growth potential.

- None of the far larger US retailers saw that Sam Walton of Wal-Mart was tapping an inexhaustible market for discount stores serving smaller communities.

- Bill Gates in his book *The Road Ahead* was dismissive of the Internet – then clearly becoming the fastest-growing phenomenon that the world has ever seen.

Would you have perceived the four present realities from which a greatly changed future sprang? If not, you have plenty of company. The majority, silent or vocal, tends strongly to the side of the *status quo* – thus, the conventional wisdom. There's a simple matrix that depicts the folly of being wise. You can occupy any of six positions, with the degrees of differentiation on the left and those of quality on the right:

THE SAME/BETTER

THE SAME/SAME

THE SAME/WORSE

DIFFERENT/BETTER

DIFFERENT/SAME

DIFFERENT/WORSE

It doesn't take a minute's thought to see that being different and better is the strongest strategy. In product terms, that gives you a Unique Sales Proposition, a reason why the customer should buy from you and nobody else (see Chapter 1: Seizing The Opportunity). In individual terms, the USP is what differentiates you – to your advantage – from the other applicants for the job, or the venture capital, or the promotion, or the assignment, or whatever. Time and again, the successful entrepreneur is the man or woman who goes against the grain – the maverick member of the unconventional minority.

Bill Gates is assuredly such a person. The fact that he saw the error of his Internet ways, just in time, and totally recast Microsoft's strategy for the new age, is a textbook example of brilliant Encore Management. The company was still most comfortably placed above Point A on the Sigmoid Curve. It had the intellectual 'bandwidth' – and the necessary billions of dollars – to turn its strategy upside-down. Gates also had a supreme means of differentiation: his Explorer browser – free and bundled with Windows – crushed the rival Netscape, which lacked this defining advantage.

Above all, however, Gates let the dead bury their dead: he wasted no time on sentimentality. The US car makers referred to above were in love with their 'gas-guzzling dinosaurs': in love with the false idea of their own superiority vis-à-vis the Japanese: in love, above all, with the fat profit margins earned on fat cars. All these factors blinded Detroit to the realities of their markets and the present – from which alone the future can spring. Clinging to the past is an all-too-human habit. The company stuck in the past has these unfortunate and destructive characteristics – The Terrible Trio:

1   It is unwilling to experiment or to try a variety of solutions to its problems.

2   It is inflexible and closed to the lessons of current experience.

3   It is bowed down by the weight of tradition.

Human beings share these weaknesses to a considerable extent, but with one most extraordinary exception; their social habits. The speed of adoption of new products and customs is mesmerizing. At one point, only rich businessmen had mobile phones: in a flash, it seemed, everybody from tycoons to teenagers (and younger) owned the devices – and used them incessantly. The successive formats of recorded sound have won the same rapid universal acceptance, while the Internet has spread like a forest fire.

Then there's fashion. Once, female midriffs were decorously covered. Suddenly, all over the globe, at all socio-economic levels, the tops got shorter, the trousers lower and (inevitably) the midriffs barer. So-called 'reality TV' (which is anything but real) became a worldwide overnight sensation, with audiences of many millions. Similar waves of change have swept the world since history began: the enormous difference today is that the range and pace of change are materially greater even than a decade ago – which historically speaking is no time at all.

Ψ

It follows that the opportunities for superb encores are infinitely more abundant. To take them, you must ensure that you and any organization for which you work avoid the Terrible Trio. These were identified by a thoughtful manager who had masterminded one of the twentieth century's most brilliant breakthroughs. He also helpfully delineated how the threesome evolve – how the company develops subtle policies and habitual modes; how it becomes more efficient, but at the price of losing flexibility and willingness to look afresh at each day's experience; how fixed routines 'are congealed in an elaborate body of written rules'.

But that's not the half of it. The unwritten rules are more powerful still. Some are good. The bad ones, though, constitute 'a choking underbrush of custom and procedure. There comes to be an accepted way to do everything. Radical approaches from past practices are ruled out. The old hand says "You have to understand how we do things round here" ... what he means is that "how we do things" is sound and respectable and the best way'.

What adds great piquancy to this plain truth is its provenance. The speaker, Peter McColough, was one of the founding giants of Xerox, and the visionary who inspired PARC, the research facility that invented most of the concepts that powered the breakthroughs of Intel and Microsoft. But Xerox failed to exploit any of PARC's brilliant inventions; failed, too, to defend its base copier market from Japanese attack. His company provides a sobering text for McColough's own question:

> 'Is it inevitable that such organizations as Xerox should have their periods of emergence, full flower of growth and prestige and then later stagnation and death?'

Readers will recognize this as a word-picture of Handy's Sigmoid Curve. It goes against my grain, though, to accept that the Curve is 'inevitable'. It is, of course, inevitable for human lives, which all emerge, blossom, decline and die. But surely, for individual and organizations alike, clever and determined Encore Management can start new and important Curves before Point B is reached? That demands, however, a special kind of SWOT analysis, forward-looking and self-aware.

- What developments could turn my/our present Strengths into Weaknesses?

- What strategies are required to forestall these Weaknesses, and thus create new Strengths?

- What Opportunities are currently visible that I/we are failing to take?

- What Threats, other than those already observed, would undermine my/our fortunes?

Tough questions again, but they had better be asked. In the end, Encore Management can only come from an encore company, one which, to quote another star entrepreneur, is geared to the future; never does it 'the way the industry does'; has 'the willingness and confidence to act on an untried approach'; and works on an argumentative philosophy of 'disagree and commit'.

Those quotes are the very opposite of McColough's Terrible Trio and go a long way towards explaining the speaker's superiority as an encore manager. He's Andy Grove of Intel, who adds that: 'If it is hard to make a success of something, it is an order of magnitude harder to sustain the success'. It is harder still to repeat success, and the greater the success, the harder the repetition.

As an individual, you can legitimately decide, like Rebecca, when enough is enough: you've climbed your equivalent of the Seven Summits, and you won't climb K2. If you are running an organization, or part of one, there are other considerations. Have you done enough to ensure that your successors will outdo you as they find new directions – solving the Encore Problem? For every Rockefeller who leaves a lasting empire, there are hundreds of tycoons who, first, hang on too long; and second, leave inferior, inadequate successors to wrestle haplessly with the Sigmoid Curve.

Leaders have a special responsibility to those they lead, whose personal futures depend heavily on the quality of the present leader. Their virtues and sins live after them. This in no way lessens the obligation on the successors to outperform their predecessors – or seek to do so. That's a more onerous task by far than that which faces the ex-boss in his or her retirement. But leading a productive and absorbing life after a career closes is no mean challenge, either.

Potentially, there will always be new summits to tackle – and conquer. Doing new things well is a wonderful target. It makes no difference whether the objective is to read *War and Peace* – at last; ride your own Harley-Davidson; start a new business with young partners; learn to paint or play the piano; or the myriad other possibilities. The great concert of life goes on until the final curtain. With good fortune, that will only come down after a last and resounding encore.

A FURTHER SUMMIT?

- At Point A on the Sigmoid Curve, take vigorous **action** to **forestall** the fateful **fall** to Point B.

- Fight on **new ground** for an Encore, rather than compete over the same old territory, BUT ...

- Ensure than any **new venture** is well within your **established zones** of competence and marketing know-how.

- Think about the **future**, intelligently and in full possession of all **relevant facts** about the **present**.

- Aim to be '**different** and **better**', arming yourself with several Unique Selling Propositions.

- **Review** the organization's written and (especially) **unwritten rules** periodically – and **remove** as many as you can.

- Don't do it 'the way everybody else does'; have the will, wit and self-confidence to **experiment** with the new.

- Be **flexible** and open to the lessons of **current experience** at all times.

- Mark well Andy Grove's words: 'If it is **hard** to make a **success** of something, it is an order of magnitude **harder** to **sustain** the success,' BUT ...

- Bear in mind that the **upward climb** is one which anyone can achieve and enjoy.

Postscript

John Barry returned to Everest and climbed to the summit in May 2000.

Dr Ginette Harrison completed the Seven Summits with an ascent of Vinson in December 1995. She went on to climb a total of five 8,000m peaks, including Kangchenjunga, on which she made the first female ascent. Sadly, she died in an avalanche on Dhaulagiri – a Himalayan peak that would have been her sixth 8,000m summit – on 24 October 1999.

Index